On
Nietzsche

On
Nietzsche

by

GEORGES BATAILLE

Translated by Bruce Boone
Introduction by Sylvère Lotringer

PARAGON HOUSE
St. Paul, Minnesota

First paperback edition, 1994.
First American edition, 1992

Published in the United States by

Paragon House
2700 University Avenue West
St. Paul, MN 55114

Originally published in French under the title *Sur Nietzsche*.
Copyright © Éditions Gallimard 1945
English translation copyright © 1992 Paragon House

Manufactured in the United States of America

Library of Congress Cataloging-in-Publication Data

Bataille, Georges, 1897–1962.
[Sur Nietzsche. English]
On Nietzsche / by Georges Bataille ; translated by Bruce Boone ;
introduction by Sylvère Lotringer.—1st American ed.
p.   cm.
Translation of: Sur Nietzsche.
ISBN 1-55778-644-5 (pbk)
ISBN 1-55778-325-X (HC)
1. Nietzsche, Friedrich Wilhelm, 1844–1900.   I. Title.
B3317.B41513   1992
193—dc20   91-26664
                                                 CIP

This edition is published with the help of the French Ministry of Culture.

Contents

Furiously Nietzschean

An Introduction by Sylvère Lotringer

GEORGES BATAILLE wasn't a "regular" philosopher like Hegel or Sartre. He was diffident of concepts, resilient to systems and deeply suspicious of language. Bataille never developed ideas that he didn't back up with his life. One shouldn't expect, therefore, *On Nietzsche* to be a traditional commentary. It is, rather, an attempt by Bataille to circumscribe what he recognized in Nietzsche as his own.

Nietzsche was a major influence in Bataille's life. In 1915 Bataille converted to Catholicism after leaving his father, blind and syphilitic, in the hands of the Germans. It is Nietzsche who rescued him, at age twenty-three, from this crisis, turning him as passionately against religion. All through the years that preceded World War II, Bataille was among the very few who tried to clear Nietzsche from the stain of National Socialism. In various issues of *Acephale*, he proved, text in hand, that Nietzsche was "the least patriot[ic] of all Germans, and the least German of the Germans," a sovereign thinker especially hostile to pan-German anti-Semitism, this "shameless humbug of races."

Reclaiming Nietzsche from the Nazis was also a way of validating his own fascination for violence and fanaticism, a "fundamental aspiration of humanity," he said, that the fascists misappropriated. In the Spring of 1939, while everyone was praying for peace, Bataille could be found hailing the war as "something ordinary life lacked— something that causes fear and prompts horror and anguish," like falling off a rooftop, or a volcano erupting.

Alas, war proved a disappointment. Beset by tuberculosis, Bataille was forced to take a leave from his job as a librarian and spend most of the wartime in the country. Never had he been more isolated—more disoccupied—than during the German occupation.

Bataille found the war *boring*.

For Bataille, however, being bored was just a way of being. Only anguish—extreme anguish—could violate the limits of being and bring intensity back into his life. This is what Bataille trained himself to experience on his own, methodically, suffocating himself into a trance with images of torture and dismemberment. These spells of deep anguish and "somber incandescence" were haltingly chronicled in his wartime writings.

The period between 1941 and 1944 was, paradoxically, one of the most prolific in Bataille's lifetime. After *Madame Edwarda*, a story of intense erotic mysticism, he wrote, and published, *Inner Experience*, *Guilty*, and *On Nietzsche*, all blinding statements made of fragments and aphorisms, journal entries, quotes and feverish notes. For a while Bataille envisaged including these three volumes in a magnum opus, *The Atheological Summa*, an ambitious project, which was never completed. Now that he was released from the political fervor of the prewar years, he had come to view any effort (any action) as a symptom of "decline," a betrayal of the "summit." His thoughts only thrived in the passing instant. No wonder they didn't hold together—any more than Nietzsche's own aphorisms.

"Except for (a few) exceptions," Bataille wrote, "my company on earth is mostly Nietzsche . . ." Not an easy thing to do, keeping Nietzsche company. Few would take up the challenge—or deserve the try. "Intimacy with great thinking is unbearable," Nietzsche warned. "I seek and make appeal to whom I can communicate such thinking without bringing about their deaths."

Disciples are too weak *not* to die when confronted with an excessive experience. Bataille was ready to die, but *without dying from it*. Dying and coming back was what Bataille thought "communication" is about. A ritual sacrifice where the crime is shared; outer violence turned inward, destroying the limits of being. Sacrificing discourse for a more intense form of communication was something Nietzsche seemed to have been able to do effortlessly. Bataille was less fortunate: "The neurotic has only a single way out AND MUST RISK HIMSELF." Bataille's own "disorderly method" was a deliberate gamble with madness: *a will to chance. . . .*

Bataille started his essay on a startling admission: "Motivating this writing—as I see it—is fear of going crazy."

On Nietzsche: a tale of unsatisfied desire?

As could be expected, Bataille quoted Nietzsche extensively—although not to the point of disappearing entirely behind his mentor's text, as happens in *Memorandum*, a collage of Nietzsche's later writings Bataille also published in 1944, to celebrate the centenary of Nietzsche's birth. Yet Nietzsche's *Genealogy of Morals* is hardly present anywhere, a curious oversight considering that *On Nietzsche* set itself as a goal to "pose and resolve intimate problems of morality."

Was that something deliberate on Bataille's part?

In his *Genealogy*, Nietzsche probed the origin of moral ideas, questioning the worth of the notions of good and evil in "our sinister European civilization." Bataille, apparently, followed suit. Right from the start, he warned the reader that he intended to show the opposition between good and evil "under another light." Yes, but which light? Nietzsche's light? Nietzsche never treated morality as an "intimate" problem; nor did he put much faith in man's interior world, the breeding ground for that terrible sickness: bad conscience. Nietzsche's main concern wasn't with man's soul, but with the disastrous effect it may have on *the human species* as a whole, preventing it from reaching "the peak of magnificence of which he is capable." Would Nietzsche, in any case, have examined the question of ethics, not in terms of action but, as Bataille did, "in reference to being—or beings"? In the first essay of the *Genealogy*, Nietzsche dismissed in advance those "changelings" called *subjects* as mere linguistic fallacy. There is no being, he wrote, "behind the doing, acting, becoming . . . the doing is everything." (*Genealogy of Morals*, New York: Anchor Books, 1956, p. 179)

It's under an entirely different light, therefore, that Bataille explored the question of morality—the light of *inner experience*. And yet Bataille didn't consider that radical shift a betrayal. Nietzsche, he said, expressed "an extreme, unconditional human yearning . . . *independently of moral goals or of serving God*," but he couldn't always maintain himself at this summit. Although indifferent to all political stakes, he couldn't always reach beyond the stage of action which necessarily "suppresses our being as entirety." Bataille, in short, offered to supplement Nietzsche's occasional failings by drawing out *within himself* the consequences of Nietzsche's doctrine.

Memorandum similarly addressed the reader "who *would seek the consequences*." Deliberately discarding Nietzsche's most well-known themes (the will to power and eternal return) Bataille indicated what he considered the "crestline" of Nietzsche's tragic thought: the ecstatic revelation of the impossible which ruins the separation between subject and object. So far, Bataille wrote, morals had been leading from one point to the next, setting up a goal and giving the itinerary. With Nietzsche this was no longer the case. Morality now led nowhere. This realization could drive one to anguish, ecstasy, madness or dereliction, yet it constituted the supreme moral experience, "the disarming freedom of meaninglessness and an empty glory."

No one, Bataille claimed, ever dared to face this total liberation of all human possibilities.

"EXCEPT FOR ME? (I'm oversimplifying)."

This is what *On Nietzsche* is about: pushing Nietzsche's doctrine down to its most extreme consequences—the *death of the spirit*, which Nietzsche himself never actually condoned. "Of this mental void," Bataille recognized, "Nietzsche gave neither an external description nor analysis. While my destiny was such that IN SPITE OF MYSELF I slowly sketch erosion and ruin. Could I have avoided it? Everything in me wanted it that way. . . ." (*Oeuvres Completes*, VI. Paris: Gallimard, 1973, p. 428)

Bataille never oversimplified. He did much worse: he kept raising the ante to an *impossible* height. Going all the way to the top of the pyramid, like Hegel, so he could hurl himself down to the bottom, a violent, paroxysmic gesture all the more fascinating for being empty of all content.

To be a Christian, a Revolutionary, even a Nietzschean was never enough for Bataille, who ached to be a saint, a renegade, a mystic. Occupying God's place was where the prestige was the strongest. Bataille was "furiously Christian" because God still had to be sacrificed.

Furiously political, Bataille had moved to the "ultra-left" simultaneously denouncing capitalism, reformism, parliamentarism, socialism and fascism, a truly impossible position. It was the same unconditional fanaticism that led him to become *furiously Nietzschean*.

In March 1944 Bataille presented the most theoretical part of *On Nietzsche* ("Summit and Decline," provocatively retitled "Discussion on Sin") to an assembly of philosophers, some of them Christians, like Gabriel Marcel. The gathering also included two major intellectual figures, Jean Hippolyte and Jean-Paul Sartre. (Sartre, whom Bataille met for the first time, had recently published a massive attack on *Inner Experience*, branding Bataille a "New Mystic.")

Why sin? Hippolyte asked, noting a Christian ambiguity in Bataille's speech. When you talk about sin, Sartre charged, I have the feeling that you mean something entirely different.

Bataille recognized flatly that he used the notion of sin simply "because it refers to a condition experienced with a great intensity."

"That changes everything!" Sartre exclaimed.

It did. Bataille, in essence, reformulated the question of morality in terms of what he considered the *moral summit*: sacrifice. A ritual violence that not only violated the integrity of being, but simultaneously transgressed the identity of language. The distinction between good and evil, operative in the context of "vulgar morality," was therefore inadequate to express intense experiences that tore beings apart. In Bataille's hands, these notions became nearly interchangeable, floating signifiers simply meant to register, like flags, the communal energies and intensities liberated through calculated killing.

Every society is founded on a crime committed collectively, but the deed (the anguish and revulsion it provokes) is subsequently denied by those who most benefited from it. Complicity and denial are constitutive of morality, whose concern for utility is merely there to suture the wound. This was also true for Christianity, which recognized Evil generically, in light of redemption, but refused to acknowledge its presence at the heart of the religious experience.

"There is in Christianity," Bataille argued, "a will NOT to be guilty, a will to locate the guilt outside of the Church, to find a transcendence to man in relation to guilt." This accounted for the Church's inability to deal with Evil, except as a threat coming from the outside. Doing the Church justice "in total hostility," Bataille assumed guilt and anguish as his own, daring Christianity to experience Christ's sacrifice as the equivocal expression of Evil.

Bataille was actually authenticating with his own life an invention that the Church had failed to acknowledge: of a consciousness free enough to devise its own punishment, strong enough to turn its intimate suffering into a triumphant affirmation of guilt.

Bataille didn't need to quote Nietzsche's *Genealogy* in his essay on Nietzsche any more than Foucault in his *Discipline and Punish*. Foucault, because he used the *Genealogy* as a tool; Bataille, because he turned himself into one.

Did it mean that Bataille, as a self-appointed genealogist of the soul, was immune from Nietzsche's devastating (but compassionate) attack on all the reactive forces triumphant in the world?

"Others resist their anguish . . . I accept it," Bataille wrote, exposing himself bare-chested to Nietzsche's indictment. But this is precisely how depreciation of life comes about. Turning resentment into bad conscience; matching guilt with suffering; claiming guilt as inner experience (GUILTY). All this with a perverse twist: anguish was the threshold to ecstasy, which Bataille equated with madness and sacrifice:

"I just looked at the two photographs of torture that I own. I have become nearly accustomed to these images: one of them, though, is so horrible that I couldn't help feeling weak.

"I had to stop writing. I went, as I often do, to sit by the open window: I was hardly seated when I felt carried away by some sort of ecstatic movement. Now I can't doubt anymore, as I painfully did yesterday, that such a state is more desirable than erotic *volupté*. I don't see anything: *this* is neither visible nor tangible in any way I can imagine. THIS makes it painful and heavy not to die. . . ." (*OC*, VI, p. 299)

Bataille, a "virtuoso of guilt," a master at arousing excessive emotions that shake the human soul loose from its joints? At first sight, ascetic procedures seem hardly compatible with Bataille's excessive eroticism. Yet lust may well be one of the many palliatives to morbidity, a way of making life, as Nietzsche said, "once again a highly interesting business."

Christianity certainly became a tedious business after forsaking the sense of sacrifice. "Boredom," Bataille pointed out, "has to do with the exclusion of guilt, with the complete separation between Christianity and the world of sin. . . ." Can guilt really be a cure when anguish keeps infecting the wound?

Nietzsche diagnosed the inner split found in the ascetic priest who pits life against life not in order to destroy it, but is rather "fighting tooth and nail" for its preservation. "The situation, then," he concluded, "is exactly the opposite from what the worshippers of that ideal believe it to be." (*GM*, p. 256) Asceticism is a desperate struggle *against death*, against boredom and exhaustion, an attempt to counter "the persistent morbidity of civilized man" by taking away from active forces a part of their restorative power.

Reappropriating Nietzsche, the philosopher with a thousand eyes, has never been a very difficult thing to do, starting with the crude falsifications of the Nazis. Any reading is an interpretative act anyway, without which there would be nothing to see. It all depends, though, on the kind of forces that are put into play, and the nature of the will that is mobilized. The will to ecstasy, undoubtedly, is a force—but can this force be truly affirmative when its triumph means meaninglessness?

"Nietzsche's work," Bataille admitted, "has little to do with mystical investigations. Yet Nietzsche experienced some form of ecstasy and he said it."

Nietzsche, in the *Genealogy*, certainly paid his respects to those "sportsmen of sanctity" who manage to overcome their deep physiological depression through rigorous training. He also said that regimens of this kind, from the mystics of Mount Athos to the "voluptuous inundations and ecstasies" of St. Teresa of Avila, may lead to all kinds of mental disorders.

But wasn't that precisely the kind of disorder Bataille feared (longed for) to get even closer to Nietzsche's madness?

On the eve of the war, Bataille advocated the formation of a "secret society" capable of empowering myths anew in order to rescue "*total* existence" from empty fragmentation. This attempt to found a sacred sect (by ritually sacrificing one of its members), one of the most bewildering episodes in French intellectual history, ended in failure. *On Nietzsche* was Bataille's renewed attempt to forge a community of solitaries "tragically engaged in their secret debates." But this community had a price: *Nietzsche was sacrificed to Bataille's own will to nothingness.*

Nietzsche, though, has the last word: "Man," he said, "would sooner have the void for his purpose than be void of purpose. . . ." (*GM*, p. 299)

Walking through the woods, along Silvaplana Lake, Nietzsche stopped near a huge rock erected like a pyramid, not far from Surjlev. He was laughing and trembling. "I imagine myself arriving by the side of the lake," Bataille went on, "and imagining him, I cry."

Nietzsche's eyes were often inflamed because he cried too much. These were "not sentimental tears, mind you," he warned us, "but tears of joy." Bataille's tears were infinitely more Pascalian. Everyone, including Sartre, noticed the gloomy outlook of Bataille's much touted—self-touted—laughter. Nietzsche's laughter, Sartre wrote, is lighter; Bataille's is "bitter and strained. . . . He tells us that he laughs, he doesn't make us laugh." ("Un Nouveau Mystique," *Cahiers du Sud*, February 1943)

A small point, apparently, but one that cut deep. Actually, Bataille was rather piqued. "I talked about laughter," he said during the discussion, "and I was depicted [by Sartre] as having a hollow laughter. . . . This kind of laughter is the most foreign to my own."

Everyone in the audience praised the authenticity of Bataille's voice, an unusual feature in philosophers. But no one heard his laughter. "You can never hear laughter in the Bible," Bataille remarked curtly.

The end of the debate, significantly, turned around Nietzsche's laughter. "Like him," Bataille said, "I'm having fun laughing at people on the shore from a disabled ship."

Jean Hippolyte: "It's Zarathustra's laughter."

Georges Bataille: "If you like. I'm surprised, in any case, that some people find it so bitter."

Jean Hippolyte: "Not bitter."

Georges Bataille: "To tell the truth, I'm unhappy myself."

Gabriel Marcel: "It's a story that ended badly. . . . Simple historical reference."

Georges Bataille: "So what?"

Gabriel Marcel: "Did Nietzsche still laugh in Torino?"

Maurice de Gandillac: "We're not talking about the laughter in Torino."

Georges Bataille: "What does anything mean at that point anyway?" (*OC*, VI, p. 359)

Of Bataille's community of philosophers, only a parodic scene comes to mind. It happened in the Spring of 1944, in Bataille's Paris apartment, while total war was pounding over Europe:

"We were dancing face to face in a *potlatch* of absurdity—the philosopher Sartre and me.
I remember whirling about, dancing.
Jumping, stomping down the wooden floor.
Acting rebellious—like a fool."

Bataille, Nietzsche's fool?

Enter GIOVANNI *with a heart at the end of his dagger.*

GIOVANNI: Be not amaz'd; if your misgiving hearts
Shrink at an idle sight, what bloodless fear
Of coward passion would have seized your senses,
Had you beheld the rape of life and beauty
Which I have acted!—my sister, oh my sister!

FLORIO: Ha! what of her?

GIOVANNI: The glory of my deed
Dark'ned the mid-day sun, made noon as night.

—FORD, *'Tis Pity She's a Whore*

Preface

1

Do you seek warmth of me? Come not too close, I counsel, or your hands may burn. For look! My ardor exceeds the limit, and I barely restrain the flames from leaping from my body!

—1881–86*

Motivating this writing—as I see it—is fear of going crazy.

I'm on fire with painful longings, persisting in me like unsatisfied desire.

In one sense, my tension is a crazy urge to laugh, not so different in its way from the ravaging passions of Sade's heroes but close, too, to the tensions of the martyrs and saints . . .

On this score, I have few doubts—my delirium brings out human qualities. Though by implication an imbalance is there as well—and distressingly I'm deprived of all rest. I'm ablaze, disoriented—and finally empty. Whatever great or necessary actions come to mind, none answers to this feverishness. I'm speaking of moral concerns—of discovering some object that surpasses all others in value!

Compared to the moral ends normally advanced, the object I refer to is incommensurable. Moral ends seem deceptive and lusterless. Still, only moral ends translate to acts (aren't they determined as a demand for definite acts?).

---

*Quotations from Nietzsche are given without the author's name, and the dates mentioned refer to posthumous notes.

The truth is, concern about this or that limited good can sometimes lead to the summit I am approaching. But this occurs in a
roundabout way. And moral ends, in this case, are distinct from any
excesses they occasion. States of glory and moments of sacredness
(which reveal incommensurability) surpass results intentionally
sought. Ordinary morality puts these results on the same footing as
sacrificial ends. Sacrifice explores the grounding of worlds, and the
destruction realized discloses a sacrificial laceration. All the same, it's
for the most banal reasons that sacrifice is celebrated. Morality ad-
dresses our good.

(Things changed in appearance when God was represented as a
unique and veritable end. Now, some will say the incommensurability of which I speak is simply God's transcendence. But
for me transcendence is avoiding my object. Nothing radically
changes when instead of human satisfaction, we think of the satisfaction of some heavenly being! God's person displaces the problem
and does not abolish it. It simply introduces confusions. When so
moved or when circumstances require—in regard to God—being
will grant itself an incommensurable essence. *By serving God and
acting on his behalf* we reduce him to ordinary ends that exist in
action. *If he were situated beyond, there would be nothing to be done on
his behalf.*)

2

An extreme, unconditional human yearning was expressed for the
first time by Nietzsche *independently of moral goals or of serving God.*

Nietzsche can't really define it, but it motivates him and it's what
he unreservedly makes his own. Of course, ardor that doesn't address a dramatically articulated moral obligation is a paradox. In this
context there is no preaching or action that is possible. The result
from this is something disturbing. If we stop looking at states of ardor
as simply preliminary to other and subsequent conditions grasped as
beneficial, the state I propose seems a pure play of lightning, merely
an empty consummation. Lacking any relation to material benefits
such as power or the growth of the state (or of God or a Church or a

party), this consuming can't even be comprehended. *It appears that the positive value of loss can only be given as gain.*

Nietzsche wasn't entirely clear on this difficulty. He must have known he failed, and in the end knew he was a voice crying out in the wilderness. To be done with obligation and *good*, to expose the lying emptiness of morality, he destroyed the effective value of language. Fame came late to him, and as it did, he thwarted it. His expectations went unanswered.

Today it appears that I ought to say his readers and his admirers show him scant respect (he knew this and said so).* *Except for me?* (I am oversimplifying). Still . . . to try, as he asked, to follow him is to be vulnerable to trials and tribulations similar to his.

This total liberation of human possibility as he defined it, of all possibilities is, of course, the only one to remain untried (I repeat by way of simplification, except perhaps by me?). At the current historical juncture, I suppose each conceivable teaching preached has had its effect. Nietzsche in turn conceived and preached a new doctrine, he gathered disciples, aspired to found an order. He had contempt for what he received—vulgar praise!

I think it is appropriate today to state my confusion. Within myself I tried to draw out consequences of a lucid doctrine impelling and attracting me to it as if to the light. I've reaped a harvest of anguish and, most often, a feeling of going under.

3

Going under, I don't abandon the yearnings I spoke of. Or rather they don't abandon me. And I die. Even dying doesn't silence me: at least that's my belief. And I want those I love also to undergo—to go under also.

In the essence of humanness a fierce impulse seeks autonomy, the freedom to be. Naturally, freedom can be understood in many different ways—but is it any wonder that people today are dying for it? On my own, I'll have to face the same difficulties as Nietzsche—putting

*See below, p. 7.

God and the good behind him, though all ablaze with the ardor possessed by those who lay down their lives for God or the good. The discouraging loneliness he described oppresses me. But breaking away from moral entities gives such truth to the air I breathe, I'd rather live as a cripple or die than fall back into slavery!

4

As I write, I'll admit that moral investigations that aim to surpass the good lead first of all to disorder. There's no guarantee yet I'll pass the test. Founded on painful experience, this admission allows me to dismiss those who, in attacks on or exploitations of Nietzsche, confuse his position with that of Hitler.

*"In what height is my abode? Ascending, I've never counted the steps leading to myself—and where the steps cease, that is where I have my roof and my abode."**

Thus a demand is expressed, one not directed at some comprehensible good—but all the more consuming to the degree that it's experienced.

I lose patience with crude equivocations. It's frightening to see thought reduced to the propaganda level—thought that remains comically unemployable, opening to those whom the void inspires. According to some critics, Nietzsche exercised a great influence on his times. I doubt it: No one expected him to dismiss moral laws. But above all he took no political stance and, when pressed to, refused to choose a party, disturbed at the possibility of either a right- or left-wing identification. The idea of a person's subordinating his or her thinking to a cause appalled him.

His strong feelings on politics date from his falling out with Wagner and from his disillusionment with Wagner's German grossness—Wagner the socialist, the Francophobe, the anti-Semite . . . The spirit of the Second Reich, especially in its pre-Hitlerite tendencies—the emblem of which is anti-Semitism—is what he most despised. Pan-German propaganda made him sick.

*The Will to Power

"I like creating from *tabula rasa*," he wrote. "It is in fact one of my ambitions to be imputed a great scorner of the Germans. Even at the age of twenty-six, I expressed the suspicions that their nature had aroused in me" (*Third Jeremiad*). "To me, there is something impossible about the Germans, and if I try to imagine a type repellent to all my instincts, it's always a German who comes to mind" (*Ecce Homo*). For the clear-sighted, at a political level Nietzsche was a prophet, foretelling the crude German fate. He was the first to give it in detail. He loathed the impervious, vengeful, self-satisfied foolishness that took hold of the German mind after 1870, which today is being spent in Hitlerite madness. No more deadly error has ever led a whole people astray and so terribly ordained it for destruction. But taking leave of the (by now) dedicated crowd, he went his way, refusing to be part of orgies of "self-satisfaction." His strictness had its consequences. Germany chose to ignore a genius so unwilling to flatter her. It was only Nietzsche's notoriety abroad that belatedly secured the attention of his people . . . I know of no better example of the wall of incomprehension existing between one person and his or her country: for fifteen years a whole nation remaining deaf to that voice—isn't this a serious matter? As witnesses to that destruction, we ought to look in admiration at the fact that while Germany took the path leading to the worst developments, one of the best and most passionate Germans turned away from his country with feelings of horror and uncontrollable disgust. Taken all round in any case, in their attempts to evade him as much as in their aberrations, doesn't hindsight let us see something vulnerable in this inconclusiveness?

In their opposition to each other, at last both Nietzsche and Germany will probably experience the same fate: both equally, aroused by demented hopes, though not to any purpose. Beyond this tragically pointless confusion, lacerations, and hatreds governed their relations. The resemblances are insignificant. If the habit of not taking Nietzsche seriously did not exist, the habit of doing what most annoyed him, giving him a cursory reading to exploit him, *without even putting aside positions which he saw as being incompatible with his*, his teaching would be seen for what it is—the most violent of solvents. To view this teaching as supporting causes it actually discredits not only insults it but rides roughshod over it—showing that his readers know nothing at all about what they claim to like. To try, as I have, to push the possibilities of his teaching to the limit is to become, like Nietzsche, a field of infinite contradictions. Following his paradoxical doctrines, you are forced to see yourself as excluded from participating in current causes. You'll eventually see that solitude is your only lot.

5

In the helter-skelter of this book, I didn't develop my views as theory. In fact, I even believe that efforts of that kind are tainted with ponderousness. Nietzsche wrote "with his blood," and criticizing or, better, *experiencing* him means pouring out one's lifeblood.

I wrote hoping my book would appear in time for the centenary of his birth (October 15, 1844). I wrote from February through August, counting on the German retreat to make publication possible. I began with a theoretical statement of the problem (this is part 2, p. 29), but that short section is essentially only the account of a personal experience, an experience which continued for twenty years and came to be weighted in fear. It might prove useful here to dispel an ambiguity. There exists an idea of Nietzsche as the philosopher of a "will to power," the idea that this is how he saw himself and how he was accepted. I think of him more as a philosopher of *evil*. For him the attraction and *value* of evil, it seems to me, gave significance to what he intended when he spoke of power. Otherwise, how can passages like this be explained? "WET BLANKET. A: You're a wet blanket, and everybody knows it! B: Obviously! I'm dampening an enthusiasm that encourages belonging to some party, which is what parties won't forgive" (*Gay Science*).

That observation, among many others, doesn't in any way square with the type of practical conduct or politics derived from the "will to power" principle. In his lifetime Nietzsche had a distinct dislike for anything the expression of that will produced. If he was drawn, felt it necessary, even, to trample on received morality it's equally certain that methods of oppression (the police) aroused his disgust too. He

justified his hatred of the good as a condition for freedom itself.
Personally, and with no illusions concerning the impact of this attitude, I am opposed to all forms of coercion—but this doesn't keep
me from seeing *evil* as an object of moral exploration. Because evil is
the opposite of a constraint that on principle is practiced with a view
toward good. Of course evil isn't what a hypocritical series of misunderstandings makes it out to be: isn't it essentially a concrete *freedom*,
the uneasy breaking of a taboo?

Anarchy bothers me, particularly run-of-the-mill doctrines apolo-
gizing for those commonly taken to be criminals. *Gestapo* practices
now coming to light show how deep the affinities are that unite the
underworld and the police. It is people who hold nothing sacred
who're the ones most likely to torture people and cruelly carry out the
orders of a coercive apparatus. I can only feel intense dislike for
muddled thinkers who confusedly demand all rights for the individual. An individual's limit is not represented simply by the rights of
another individual but even more by rights of the *masses*. We are all
inextricably bound up with the masses, participating in their innermost sufferings and their victories. And in our innermost being, we
form part of a living group—though we are no less alone, for all that,
when things go wrong.

As a means to triumph over significant difficulties of this kind and
over the opposition between individual and collective or good and
evil, over the exasperating contradictions from which, generally
speaking, we are able to disentangle ourselves mostly through
denial—it seems to me that only certain chance movements, or the
audacity that comes from taking chances, will freely prevail. Chance
represents a way of going beyond when life reaches the outer limits of
the possible and gives up. Refusing to pull back, never looking
behind, our uninhibited boldness discovers that solutions develop
where cautious logic is baffled. So that it was only *with my life* that I
wrote the Nietzsche book that I had planned—a book in which I
intended to pose and resolve intimate problems of morality.

Only my life, only its ludicrous resources, only these made a quest
for the grail of chance possible for me. Chance, as it turned out,
corresponded to Nietzsche's intentions more accurately than power

could. Only "play" gave me the possibility of exploring the far reaches of possibility and not prejudicing the results, of giving to the future alone and its free occurrence the power usually assigned to choosing sides (which is only a form of the past). In a sense my book is the day-to-day record of what turned up as the dice were thrown—without, I hasten to say, there being a lot by way of resources. I apologize for the truly comical year of personal interests chronicled in my diary entries. They are not a source of pain, and I'm glad to make fun of myself, knowing no better way to lose myself in immanence.

6

Nonetheless, I don't want my inclination to make fun of myself or act comic to lead readers astray. The basic problem tackled in this chaotic book (chaotic because it has to be) is the same one Nietzsche experienced and attempted to resolve in his work—the problem of the whole human being.

"The majority of people," he wrote, "are a fragmentary, exclusive image of what humanity is; you have to add them up to get humanity. In this sense, whole eras and whole peoples have something fragmentary about them; and it may be necessary for humanity's growth for it to develop only in parts. It is a crucial matter therefore to see that what is at stake is always the idea of producing a synthetic humanity and that the inferior humans who make up a majority of us are only preliminaries, or preparatory attempts whose concerted play allows a *whole human being* to appear here and there like a military boundary marker showing the extent of humanity's advance." (*The Will to Power*)

But what does that fragmentation mean? Or better, what causes it if not a need to *act* that specializes us and limits us to the horizon of a particular activity? Even if it turns out to be for the general interest (which normally isn't true), the activity that subordinates each of our aspects to a specific result suppresses our being as an entirety. Whoever acts, substitutes a particular end for what he or she is, as a total being: in the least specialized cases it is the glory of the state or the triumph of a party. Every action specializes insofar as it is limited as action. A plant usually doesn't act, and isn't specialized; it's specialized when gobbling up flies!

I cannot exist *entirely* except when somehow I go beyond the stage of action. Otherwise I'm a soldier, a professional, a man of learning, not a "total human being." The fragmentary state of humanity is basically the same as the choice of an object. When you limit your desires to possessing political power, for instance, you act and know what you have to do. The possibility of failure isn't important—and right from the start, you insert your existence advantageously into time. Each of your moments becomes *useful*. With each moment, the possibility is given you to advance to some chosen goal, and your time becomes a march toward that goal—what's normally called living. Similarly, if salvation is the goal. Every action makes you a fragmentary existence. I hold onto my nature as an entirety only by refusing to act—or at least by denying the superiority of time, which is reserved for action.

Life is whole only when it isn't subordinate to a specific object that exceeds it. In this way, the essence of entirety is freedom. Still, I can't choose to become an entire human being by simply fighting for freedom, even if the struggle for freedom is an appropriate activity for me—because within me I can't confuse the state of entirety with my struggle. It's the positive practice of freedom, not the negative struggle against a particular oppression, that has lifted me above a mutilated existence. Each of us learns with bitterness that to struggle for freedom is first of all to alienate ourselves.

I've already said it: the practice of freedom lies within evil, not beyond it, while the struggle for freedom is a struggle to conquer a *good*. To the extent that life is entire within me, I can't distribute it or let it serve the interests of a good belonging to someone else, to God or myself. I can't acquire anything at all: I can only give and give unstintingly, without the gift ever having as its object anyone's interest. (In this respect, I look at the other's good as deceptive, since if I will that good it's to find my own, unless I identify it as my own. Entirety exists within me as exuberance. Only in empty longing, only in an unlucky desire to be consumed simply by the desire to burn with desire, *is entirety wholly what it is.* In this respect, entirety is also longing for laughter, longing for pleasure, holiness, or death. Entirety lacks further tasks to fulfill.)

7

You have to experience a problem like this to understand how strange it really is. It's easy to argue its meaning by saying, Infinite tasks are imposed on us. Precisely in the present. That much is obvious and undeniable. Still, it is at least equally true that human entirety or totality (the inevitable term) is making its initial appearance now. For two reasons. The first, negative, is that specialization is everywhere, and emphasized alarmingly. The second is that in our time over-whelming tasks nonetheless appear *within their exact limits.*

In earlier times the horizon couldn't be discerned. The object of seriousness was first defined as the good of the city, although the city was confused with the gods. The object thereafter became the salva-tion of the soul. In both cases the goal of action, on the one hand, was some limited and comprehensible end, and on the other, a totality defined as inaccessible in this world (transcendent). Action in mod-ern conditions has precise ends that are completely adequate to the possible, and human totality no longer has a mythic aspect. Seen as accessible in all that surrounds us, totality becomes the fulfillment of tasks as they are defined materially. So that totality is remote, and the tasks that subordinate our minds also fragment them. Totality, how-ever, is still discernible.

A totality like this, necessarily aborted by our work, is nonethe-less offered by that very work. Not as a goal, since the goal is to change the world and give it human dimensions. But as the inevita-ble result. As change comes about, humanity-attached-to-the-task-of-changing-the-world, which is only a single and fragmentary aspect of humanity, will itself be changed to humanity-as-entirety. For humanity this result seems remote, but *defined* tasks describe it: It doesn't transcend us like the gods (the sacred city), nor is it like the soul's afterlife; it is in the immanence of "humanity-attached . . ." We can put off thinking about it till later, though it's still contiguous to us. If human beings can't yet be consciously aware of it in their common existence, what separates them from this notion isn't that they are human instead of divine, nor the fact of not being dead: It's the duties of a particular moment.

Similarly, a man in combat must only think (provisionally) of driving back the enemy. To be sure, situations of calm during even the most violent wars give rise to peacetime interests. Still, such matters immediately appear minor. The toughest minds will join in these moments of relaxation as they seek a way to put aside their seriousness. In some sense they're wrong to do so. Since isn't seriousness essentially *why* blood flows? And that's inevitable. For how could seriousness *not* be the same as blood? How could a free life, a life unconstrained by combat, a life disengaged from the necessities of action and no longer fragmented—how could such a life *not* appear frivolous? In a world released from the gods and from any interest in salvation, even "tragedy" seems a distraction, a moment of relaxation within the context of goals shaped by activity alone.

More than one advantage accrues when human "reason for being" comes in *the back way*. So the total person is first disclosed in immanence in areas of life that are lived frivolously. A life like this—a frivolous life—can't be taken seriously. Even if it is deeply tragic. And that is its liberating prospect—it acquires the worst simplicity and nakedness. Without any guile I'm saying, I feel grateful to those whose serious attitudes and life lived at the edge of death define me as an empty human being and dreamer (there are moments when I'm on their side). Fundamentally, an entire human being is simply a being in whom transcendence is abolished, from whom there's no separating anything now. An entire human being is partly a clown, partly God, partly crazy . . . and is transparence.

8

If I want to realize totality in my consciousness, I have to relate myself to an immense, ludicrous, and painful convulsion of all of humanity. This impulse moves toward *all* meanings. It's true: sensible action (action proceeding toward some single meaning) goes beyond such incoherence, but that is exactly what gives humanity in my time (as well as in the past) its fragmentary aspect. If for a single moment I forget that meaning, will I see Shakespeare's tragical/ridiculous sum total of eccentricities, his lies, pain, and laughter; the awareness of an immanent totality becomes clear to me—but as laceration. Existence as entirety remains beyond any one meaning—and it is the conscious presence of humanness in the world inasmuch as this is nonmeaning, having nothing to do other than be what it is, no longer able to go beyond itself or give itself some kind of meaning through action.

This consciousness of totality relates to two opposed ways of using that expression. *Nonmeaning* normally is a simple negation and is said of an object to be canceled. An intention that rejects what has no meaning in fact is a rejection of the entirety of being—and it's by reason of this rejection that we're conscious of the totality of being within us. But if I say *nonmeaning* with the opposite intention, in the sense of *nonsense*, with the intention of searching for an object free of meaning, I don't deny anything. But I make an affirmation in which *all life* is clarified in consciousness.

Whatever moves toward this consciousness of totality, toward this total friendship of humanness and humanity for itself, is quite correctly held to be lacking a basic seriousness. Following this path I become ridiculous. I acquire the inconsistency of all humans (humanness taken as a whole, and overlooking whatever leads to important changes). I'm not suggesting that I'm accounting for Nietzsche's illness this way (from what we know, it had some somatic basis), though it must be said, all the same, that the main impulse that leads to human entirety is tantamount to madness. I let go of good. I let go of reason (meaning). And under my feet, I open an abyss which my activity and my binding judgments once kept from me. At least the awareness of totality is first of all within me as a despair and a crisis. If I give up the viewpoint of action, my perfect nakedness is revealed to me. I have no recourse in the world, there's nothing to help me—and I collapse. No other outcome is possible, except endless incoherence, in which only chance is my guide.

9

Now clearly, such an experience of helplessness can't be effected till all other experiences have been attempted and accomplished—till all other possibilities have been exhausted. So it can't become the fact of human entirety until the last minute. Only an extremely isolated individual can attempt it in our day, as a consequence of mental confusion and at the same time an undeniable vigor. If chance is on such a person's side, the individual can determine an unforeseen balance in this incoherence. Since this audaciously easy and divine state of balance again and again translates into a profound discordancy that remains a tightrope act, I don't imagine that the "will to power" can attain such a condition in any other way. Given this, the "will to power" considered as an end is regressive. Taking such a course would return me to slavish fragmentation. I'd assign myself another duty, and the good that chooses power would control me. The divine exuberance and lightheartedness expressed in Zarathustra's laughter and dancing would be reabsorbed. And instead of happiness at the brink of the abyss, I'd be tied to weightiness, the slavishness of *Kraft durch Freude*. If we put aside the equivocations of the "will to power," the destiny Nietzsche gave humankind places him beyond laceration. There is no return, hence the profound nonviability of this doctrine. In the notes compiled in *The Will to Power*, proposals for activity and the temptation to work out a goal or politics end up as a maze. His last completed work, *Ecce Homo*, affirms absence of goals as well as the author's complete lack of a plan.* Considered from the standpoint of action, Nietzsche's work amounts to failure (one of the most indefensible!) and his life amounts to nothing—like the life of anyone who tries to put these writings into practice.

10

I want to be very clear on this: not a word of Nietzsche's work can be understood without *experiencing* that dazzling dissolution into totality,

*See below, p. 86.

without living it out. Beyond that, this philosophy is just a maze of contradictions. Or worse, the pretext for lies of omission (if, as with the Fascists, certain passages are isolated for ends disavowed by the rest of the work). I now must ask that closer attention be paid. It must have been clear how the preceding criticism masks an approval. It justifies the following definition of the entire human—*human existence as the life of "unmotivated" celebration*, celebration in all meanings of the word: laughter, dancing, orgy, the rejection of subordination, and sacrifice that scornfully puts aside any consideration of ends, property, and morality.

The preceding introduces a necessity to make distinctions. Extreme states, either individual or collective, once were motivated by ends. Some of these have lost their meaning (expiation and salvation). The search for the good of collectivities today no longer is pursued via recourse to dubious means, but directly through action. In previous conditions, extreme states came under the jurisdiction of the arts, though certain drawbacks existed. People substituted writing (fiction) for what was once spiritual life, poetry (chaotic words) for actual ecstasies. Art constitutes a minor free zone outside action, paying for its freedom by giving up the real world. A heavy price! Rare is the writer who doesn't yearn for the rediscovery of a vanished reality; but the payment required is relinquishing his or her freedom and serving propaganda. Artists who limit themselves to fiction know they aren't human entireties, though the situation isn't any different for literary propagandists. The province of the arts in a sense encompasses totality, though just the same, totality escapes it in all aspects.

Nietzsche is far from having resolved the difficulty, since Zarathustra is himself a poet, in fact a literary fiction. Only he never accepted this. Praise exasperated him. He frantically looked for a way out—in every direction. He never abandoned the watchword of *not having any end*, not serving a cause, because, as he knew, causes *pluck off the wings we fly with*. Although the absence of causes, on the other hand, pushes us into solitude, which is the sickness of a desert, the shout lost in the silence . . .

The understanding I encourage involves a similar absence of out-come and takes a similar enthusiasm for torment for granted. In this sense I think the idea of the eternal return should be reversed. It's not a promise of infinite and lacerating repetitions: It's what makes moments caught up in the immanence of return suddenly appear as ends. In every system, don't forget, these moments are viewed and given as means: Every moral system proclaims that "each moment of life ought to be *motivated*." Return *unmotivates* the moment and frees life of ends—thus first of all destroys it. Return is the mode of drama, the mask of human entirety, a human desert wherein each moment is unmotivated.

There are no two ways about it, and a choice has to be made. On one side is the desert, on the other, mutilation. Misfortune can't just be left behind like a package. Suspended in the void, extreme moments are followed by depressions that no hope can alleviate. If, however, I come to a clear awareness of what's experienced along such a path, I can give up my search for a way out where none is to be found (for that reason I've retained my criticism). Can we believe that the absence of a goal inherent in Nietzsche's outlook wouldn't have certain consequences? Inevitably, chance and the search for chance represent the single applicable recourse (to the vicissitudes he de-scribed in his book). But to proceed rigorously in such a fashion necessarily implies dissociation in the impulse itself.

Even if it's true that, as it is usually understood, a man of action can't be a human entirety, human entirety nonetheless retains the possibility of acting. Provided, however, that such action is reduced to appropriately human (or reasonable) principles and ends. Human entirety can't be transcended (that is, subdued) by action, since it would lose its totality. Nor can it transcend action (submit it to its ends), since in this way it would define itself as a motive and would enter into and be annihilated by the mechanism of motivation. It's important to distinguish between the world of motives on the one hand, that is, things making sense (rational), and the (senseless) world of non-sense on the other. Each of us sometimes belongs to one, sometimes to the other. We can consciously and clearly distinguish what is connected only in ignorance. Reason for me is limited only by itself. If we act, we stray outside the motivation of equity and a rational order of acts. Between the two worlds only a single relationship is possible: action has to be *rationally* limited by a principle of freedom.*

The rest is silence.

---

*Since the accursed fiery or mad share, or the *part maudite*, of human entireness is meted out (sponsored from outside) by reason following liberal and reasonable norms, capitalism is condemned as an irrational mode of activity. As soon as human entirety (that is, its irrationality) is able to recognize itself as outside action, or sees in every transcendent possibility a trap and loss of its totality, we will give up irrational (feudal, capitalist) dominations in the sphere of activity. Nietzsche certainly foresaw the necessity for this relinquishment without noting its cause. Human entirety can only be what it is when giving up the addiction to others' *ends*; it enslaves itself in going beyond, in limiting itself to the feudal or bourgeois spheres this side of freedom. True, Nietzsche still believed in social transcendence or hierarchy. To say that "there is nothing sacred in immanence" signifies that what once was sacred can no longer serve. The time derived from freedom is the time for laughter: "To see tragic natures go under and be able to laugh . . ." (Do we dare apply that proposition to present events—instead of involving ourselves in new moral transcendancies?) In freedom, abandon, and the immanence of laughter, Nietzsche was among the first to eliminate what still linked him (still linked his adolescent immoralism) to vulgar forms of transcendence, which remain freedoms still in chains. To choose evil is to choose freedom—"freedom, emancipation from all constraint."

PART I

Mr. Nietzsche

So let's leave Mr. Nietzsche and go on . . .
　　　　　　　　　—*Gay Science*

I

I live—if I choose to see things this way—among a curious race that sees earth, its chance events and the vast interconnectedness of animals, mammals, and insects not so much in relation to themselves—or the necessities limiting them—but in relation to the unlimited, lost, and unintelligible aspect of the skies. Theoretically, for us happy beings, Mr. Nietzsche is a secondary problem . . . Though there exists . . .

IT's OBVIOUS such happy beings aren't that much in evidence, I must quickly add.

Except for a few exceptions, my company on earth is mostly Nietzsche . . .

Blake or Rimbaud are ponderous and touchy.

Proust's limitation is his innocence, his ignorance of the winds that blow from the outside.

Nietzsche is the only one to support me: he says *we*. If *community* doesn't exist, Mr. Nietzsche is a philosopher.

"If from the *death of God*," he says speaking to *me*, "we don't fashion a major renunciation and perpetual *victory over ourselves*, we'll have to pay for that loss" (*The Will to Power*).

That sentence has a meaning—I immediately saw what it was driving at.

We can't rely on anything.

Except ourselves.

Ludicrous responsibility devolves on us, overwhelms us.

3

In every regard, right up to the present, people always have relied on each other—or God.

As I write I hear rolling thunder, moaning wind: I am watching within me, sensing noise, explosions, storms moving across the land over time. In an unlimited time, unlimited sky, traversed by crashing roars, dispensing death as simply as the heart pumps blood, I feel myself born away in sharp impulses—too violent for me right now. Through the shutters into my window comes an infinite wind, carrying with it unleashed struggles, raging disasters of the ages. And don't I too carry within me a blood rage, a blindness satisfied by the hunger to mete out blows? How I would enjoy being a pure snarl of hatred, demanding death: the upshot being no prettier than two dogs going at it tooth and nail! Though I am tired and feverish . . .

"Now the air all around is alive with the heat, earth breathing a fiery breath. Now everyone walks naked, the good and bad, side by side. And for those in love with knowledge, it's a celebration." (*The Will to Power*)

"The profoundest thinkers aren't those whose stars orbit cyclical pathways. To those who see inside themselves as if into the immense universe and who in themselves bear Milky Ways, the extreme irregularity of these constellations is well known; they lead directly to chaos and to a labyrinthine existence." (*Gay Science*)

II

AN UNLUCKY incident gives me a feeling of sin: I don't have any right to run out of luck!

Breaking the moral law was necessary to experience that urgency. (Compared to the strictness of this attitude, wasn't the old morality simple?)

Now begins a difficult and unrelenting journey—the quest for the most distant possibility.

The idea of a morality that couldn't conquer the possible beyond good, wouldn't such an idea be ridiculous?

"To deny worth, but to do what surpasses all praise or (for that matter) understanding." (*The Will to Power*)

"If we want to create, we have to credit ourselves with much more freedom than previously was given us and thus free ourselves of morality and bring liveliness to our celebrations. (Intimations of the future! To celebrate the future and not the past! To invent the myth of this future! To live in hopefulness!) Blessed moments! But then: let the curtain fall, and let us bring our thinking back to solid goals near at hand!" (*The Will to Power*)

The future: not a prolonging of the self through time but the occurrence of surpassing, going further than the limits reached.

III

. . . the heights where you find him link him in friendship to recluses, to the unrecognized of all times.

—1882–85

"RECLUSES AMONG recluses, where will we be then? Since it is certainly the case that that's where, because of science, we'll some day be. Where will human companions be found? It used to be we would look for a king, father, a judge for us all—since we needed authentic kings, fathers, judges. Later on *we'll seek a friend*, since human beings will have become splendid autonomous systems, though remaining *alone*. Mythological instinct will then go looking for *a friend*." (*The Will to Power*)

"We'll make philosophy a dangerous thing, change the idea of it, teach a philosophy that is *dangerous to life*; what better service can be rendered to philosophy? The more expensive the idea, the more it will be cherished. If we unhesitatingly sacrifice ourselves to notions of 'God,' 'Country,' and 'Freedom,' and if all of history is the smoke surrounding this kind of sacrifice, how can we show the primacy of the concept of 'philosophy' over popular concepts like 'God,' 'Country,' and 'Freedom,' except by making the former *more expensive* than the latter—showing that it demands still greater hecatombs?" (*The Will to Power*)

If it were ever entertained, this proposal might prove interesting. With no one in the offing wanting to die for it, however, Nietzsche's doctrine is null and void.

If I ever have occasion to write out my last words in blood, I'll write this: "Everything I *lived*, said, or wrote—everything I loved—I considered *communication*. How could I live my life otherwise? Living this recluse's life, speaking in a desert of isolated readers, accepting the buoyant touch of *writing*! My accomplishment, its sum total, is to have taken risks and to have my sentences fall like the victims of war now lying in the fields." I want people to laugh, shrug their shoulders, and say, "He's having fun at our expense, he's alive." True, I live on, even now am full of life, though I declare, "If you find me reluctant to take risks in this book, throw it away; if on the other hand, when you read me you find nothing to *risk yourself*, then listen: *Throughout your life* up until your death, your reading will only corrupt you . . . and you'll stink with corruption."

"THE TYPE OF MY DISCIPLES—For any of those *in whom I take an interest* I wish only suffering, abandonment, sickness, ill treatment and disgrace; I don't want them spared the profound contempt for self or the martyrdom that is mistrust of self; they haven't stirred me to pity . . ." (*The Will to Power*)

Nothing human necessitates a community of those desiring humanness. Anything taking us down that road will require combined efforts—or at least continuity from one person to the next—not limiting ourselves to the possibilities of a single person. To cut my ties with what surrounds me makes this solitude of mine a mistake. A life is only a link in the chain. I want other people to continue the experience begun by those before me *and dedicate themselves* like me and the others before me to this—*to go to the furthest reaches of the possible.*

Sentences will be consigned to museums if the emptiness in writing persists.

Currently we take pride in this—that nothing can be understood till first of all deformed, emptied of content, by one of two mechanisms—propaganda and writing!

Like a woman, possibility makes demands, makes a person go all the way.

Strolling with art lovers through the galleries and across the polished wooden floors in the museum of possibilities, inside of us we eventually kill off whatever isn't grossly political, confining it to sumptuous dated and labeled illusions.

Only when shame brings this home to us do we realize it.

To live out possibility to the utmost means many will have to change—*taking it on as something outside of them*, no longer depending on any one of them.

Nietzsche never doubted that if the possibility he recommended was going to exist, it would require community.

Desire for community was constantly on his mind.

He wrote, "Intimacy with great thinking is unbearable. I seek and call out to those to whom I can communicate such thinking without bringing about their deaths." *Without finding them*, he sought *souls who would be "deep enough."* He had to resign himself, content himself with saying: "When a challenge like this rises from the soul's depths, not to hear the sound of a reply is a terrifying experience, and possibly even the most tenacious perish from it. It freed me from my ties with living men."

Numerous observations express his suffering . . .

"You're preparing for a time when you'll have to speak. Perhaps at that point you will be ashamed of speaking, just as you sometimes are of writing. You may still have to interpret yourself—and is it possible your actions and abstentions won't suffice to *communicate* yourself? There will come a cultural era in which to read at all will be construed as bad taste; there will be no reason to blush when you are read in that future age; while at present when you are called a writer, you're insulted; and whoever praises you on account of your stories reveals a lack of tact, creating a gap between you and him; and it never crosses your mind that this glorification is in fact humiliation. I know what the present-day condition of the reader's soul is; but beware of your wish to expend efforts on that state, to go to any trouble to produce it!

"Men who possess a destiny, those who by going forth take on a destiny, the whole breed of relentless drudges, oh, don't they long for rest now and then! They yearn for the strong hearts and sturdy necks that (for a few hours at least) take away the weight pressing down upon them! But how vain that desire! . . . They wait, and nothing of what takes place around them responds to their attention. No one comes to meet them with even the smallest portion of their own suffering and excitement. No one suspects what they put into their waiting . . . Finally, further along, they learn this elementary bit of wisdom: stop waiting. And a second lesson: be congenial, be modest, take everything in stride . . . That is, be a bit more relaxed than has been the case up to now." (*The Will to Power*)

My life with Nietzsche as a companion is a community. My book is this community.

I take the following few lines very much to heart:

"I don't desire to become a saint, I prefer being taken for a fool . . . And perhaps I am a fool . . . But all the same—though not 'all the same,' since nothing has ever been as deceptive as a saint—the truth speaks from my mouth . . ."

I am not about to rip masks off anyone . . .

What do we in fact know about Mr. Nietzsche?

Constrained to sickness and silence . . . loathing the Christians . . . And we won't mention the others! . . .

And then . . . there are so few of us!

IV

Nothing speaks as vividly to our hearts as these sprightly melodies with their absolute sadness.

—1888

"You BLAME this sovereign spirit, a spirit that for the present suffices unto itself, you blame it for being well protected, for being fortified against sudden attack. You blame it for the walls surrounding it, for the mysteries within it—though still you glance curiously through the golden bars that surround its domain—fascinated and interested. For the hints of unknown perfumes are drifting mockingly across your face, disclosing something of the secret gardens and delights." (*The Will to Power*)

"There is a false appearance of cheer against which nothing can be done; but adopting it, one has to be finally satisfied with it. We who have taken refuge in *happiness*, who in a certain sense need the noon and its wild excesses of sunlight, who sit by the edge of the road to watch life go by like a procession of masqueraders or a drama wherein we go mad—doesn't it appear that we're aware of our fear of something? Something in us breaks easily. Do we fear youthful and destructive hands? Is it to avoid chance that we take refuge in life, in its brilliance, in its falsity and superficiality, in its shiny lies? If we seem lighthearted, is it from being infinitely sad? We are serious because we know something of the abyss—and is this why we erect barriers to that seriousness? We laugh within ourselves at those with a taste for melancholy, whom we suspect of lacking depth—alas, we envy them as we deride them, since we aren't happy enough to allow

10

them their delicate misery. We're compelled to flee the barest hints of sadness—our hell and our darkness are always too near. There is something we know that we dread, something we don't want to be on good terms with; the faith we have makes us tremble, its murmurings cause us to grow pale—and those who don't believe in that faith seem happy to us. We turn aside from the sight of misery, stop our ears to the lamentations of suffering; and pity would break us, if we didn't have the secret of toughening ourselves. Stay with us in your courage, oh you mocking indifference! Cool us, ye winds blowing from the glaciers! We'll no longer take things to heart—we're choosing as our supreme god and redeemer: the *mask*." (*The Will to Power*)

"The supreme cosmic discourse: 'I am cruelty, trickery,' etc., etc. Mocking our fear of assuming responsibility for mistakes (mocking a *creator*) or for any pain. More malicious than ever before etc. This is a supreme way of taking pleasure in our own work; wrecking it so as to be able to reconstruct it again and again. It's a new triumph over death, pain, obliteration." (*The Will to Power*)

" 'Be sure! From now on I will take interest only in necessity! Be sure: *amor fati* will be my supreme love!' " —There exists the possibility you'll go that far; though first you will have to show some interest in the Furies. And I declare that their serpents make me hesitate. —" 'What do you know about the Furies? The Furies, isn't that just a derogatory name for the Graces?'—He's out of his mind!" (*The Will to Power*)

"Indicating the power and confidence obtained by showing that 'I've unlearned fear'; in place of mistrust and doubt, trust our instincts; each person loving and honoring himself or herself in wisdom and even *absurdity*; partly as a fool, partly as a god; not being a figure of woe or an owl; or a serpent . . ." (*The Will to Power*)

V

What was the greatest sin at that point? Wasn't it the phrase uttered by the person who said, "Woe unto those who laugh while on this earth?"

—*Zarathustra*, "On the Superman"

"FREDERICK NIETZSCHE had always wanted to write a classical work, a history book, a system, a poem, something worthy of the old Hellenes he chose as masters. He never had been able to give form to that ambition. At the end of 1883, he had just completed an almost desperate undertaking; and the abundance and importance of these notes allow us to have some sense about the greatness of a work that remained utterly in vain. He could not provide his moral ideas with any foundation, nor could he write his tragic poem; as the two books were frustrated, his hopes disappeared. What was he? An unfortunate—capable only of short efforts, lyric songs, cries." (Daniel Halévy)

"In 1872 he sent Mademoiselle Meysenburg his incomplete series of lectures on the future of the universities: 'They make me terribly thirsty,' he said, 'but alas, they offer nothing to drink.' The same words could be applied to his poem." (Halévy)

PART II

Summit and Decline

*Here, no one will slip in
and follow you. Your
steps have of themselves
blotted out the path behind
you, and above your path
is inscribed—Impossible!*

—*Zarathustra*, "The Traveler"

THE QUESTIONS that I want to raise deal with good and evil in reference to being, or beings.

Good is given first as the good of the individual. Evil seems to be a bias that obviously acts against this or that given individual. Possibly, good is respect for individuals and evil their violation. If these judgments make sense, I can derive them from my feelings.

On the contrary, good relates to having contempt for the interest of beings in themselves. According to this secondary conception (secondary, though remaining part of the totality of emotions) evil would be the existence of individuals—insofar as this implies their separation.

Reconciliation between these conflicting forms seems simple: good would be the interest of *others*.

So there is the possibility that all morality might rest on equivocation and derives from shifts.

But before coming to the questions this raises, I will look at the opposition from another angle.

I

The crucified Christ is the most sublime of all symbols—even at present.

—1885–86

I now want to contrast, not good and evil, but the "moral summit," which is different from the good, and the "decline," which has nothing to do with evil and whose necessity determines, on the contrary, modalities of the good.

The summit corresponds to excess, to an exuberance of forces. It brings about a maximum of tragic intensity. It relates to measureless expenditures of energy and is a violation of the integrity of individual beings. It is thus closer to evil than to good.

The decline—corresponding to moments of exhaustion and fatigue—gives all value to concerns for preserving and enriching the individual. From it come rules of morality.

To begin with, I will show how the summit of Christ on the cross is an extremely equivocal expression of evil.

THE KILLING of Jesus Christ is held by Christians as a group to be evil.

It is the greatest sin ever committed.

It even possesses an unlimited nature. Criminals are not the only actors in this drama, since the fault devolves on all humans. Insofar as someone does evil (every one of us being *required* to do evil), that person puts Christ on the cross.

Pilate's executioners crucified Jesus, though the God they nailed to the cross was put to death as a sacrifice. Crime is the agent of this

17

sacrifice, a crime that sinners since Adam have infinitely committed. The loathesomeness concealed in human life (everything tainted and impossible carried in its secret places, with its evil condensed in its stench) has so successfully violated good that nothing close to it can be imagined.

The killing of Christ injures the being of God.

It looks as if creatures couldn't communicate with their Creator except through a wound that lacerates integrity.

The wound is intended and desired by God.

The humans who did this are not less guilty.

On the other hand—and this is not the least strange—the guilt is a wound lacerating the integrity of every guilty being.

In this way God (wounded by human guilt) and human beings (wounded by their own guilt with respect to God), find, if painfully, a unity that seems to be their purpose.

If human beings had kept their own integrity and hadn't sinned, God on one hand and human beings on the other would have persevered in their respective isolation. A night of death wherein Creator and creatures bled together and lacerated each other and on all sides, were challenged at the extreme limits of shame: that is what was required for their communion.

Thus "communication," without which nothing exists for us, is guaranteed by crime. "Communication" is love, and love taints those whom it unites.

In the elevation upon a cross, humankind attains a summit of evil. But it's exactly from having attained it that humanity ceases being separate from God. So clearly the "communication" of human beings is guaranteed by evil. Without evil, human existence would turn in upon itself, would be enclosed as a zone of independence: And indeed an absence of "communication"—empty loneliness—would certainly be the greater evil.

The position of human beings evokes sympathy.

They're driven to "communicate" (with both indefinite existence and themselves): the absence of "communication" (an egotistic fold-ing back into self) clearly evokes the greatest condemnation. But since "communication" can't take place without wounding or taint-ing our humanity, "communication" itself is guilty. However the good is construed, it's the good of individuals—but by wanting to attain it (at night and through evil) we are impelled to question the very individuals in relation to whom we had sought it.

A fundamental principle is expressed as follows:

"Communication" cannot proceed from one full and intact individ-ual to another. It requires individuals whose separate existence in themselves is *risked*, placed at the limit of death and nothingness;* the moral summit is the moment of risk taking, it is a being sus-pended in the beyond of oneself, at the limit of nothingness.

*For the sense of this word see appendix 5, "Nothingness, Transcendence, Immanence," p. 188.

II

---

*. . . Humans are the cruelest animals. Participants in trage-
dies, bullfights, crucifixions—until the present they've been
more at home on earth; when they invented hell, it was in fact
their paradise . . .*

                          —*Zarathustra,* "The Convalescent"

*I*T'S IMPORTANT *to me to show that with "communication" or physical
lovemaking, desire takes nothingness as its object.*

   It's the same with any "sacrifice."

Sacrifice generally, and not just the sacrifice of Jesus, seems to give
the feeling of crime;* sacrifice is on the side of evil, evil that is
necessary for good.

Moreover, sacrifice is not intelligible if not regarded as the means
by which humans once universally "communicated" among themselves and simultaneously "communicated" with the ghosts they
understood as populating hell or heaven.

To clarify the links between "communication" and sin, between
sacrifice and sin, I'll suggest that as *sovereign* desire eats away at and
feeds on our anguish, on principle this engages us in an attempt to go
beyond ourselves.

The beyond of my being is first of all nothingness. This is the
absence I discern in laceration and in painful feelings of lack: It
reveals the presence of another person. Such a presence, however, is
fully disclosed only when the *other* similarly leans over the edge of
nothingness or falls into it (dies). "Communication" only takes place

---

*See Hubert and Mauss, *Sacrifice.*

between two people who risk themselves, each lacerated and suspended, perched atop a common nothingness.

This way of understanding things gives a similar explanation to both sacrifice and the works of the flesh. In sacrifice, humans unite with a god by putting him to death: they put to death a divinity personified by a living existence, a human or animal victim (the means we have to unite with each other). Sacrifice itself and its participants are in some way identified with the victim. So, as the victim is being put to death, they lean over their own nothingness. At the same time they understand how their god is slipping into death. The victim's surrender (in holocausts, the victim is burned for that reason) coincides with the blow striking the god. The gift partly frees up a "humanity" for us, and for a brief moment human beings are free to unite with the existence of their divinity, a divinity that at the same time death has brought into existence.

III

More often than the sacred object, desire has as its object the flesh; and in carnal desire, an interplay of "communication" appears in all its stringent complexity.

In the carnal act, we taint the limit of our being even while, in the process tainting ourselves, we cross it.

T HE SOVEREIGN desire of beings is what is beyond being. Anguish is the feeling of danger related to this inexhaustible expectation.

In the realm of sensuality, a being of flesh is the object of desire. Although, in that being, what *attracts* isn't immediate being but a wound, a break in the body's integrity, the orifice of filth. This wound doesn't precisely risk life—only life's integrity and its purity. It doesn't kill, it sullies. What is disclosed in defilement doesn't differ substantially from what is revealed in death—the dead body and excreted matter are both expressive of *nothingness*, while the dead body in addition participates in filth. Excrement is the dead part of me I have to get rid of, by making it disappear, finally annihilating it. In sensuality as in death, moreover, nothingness in *itself* isn't what attracts us. What captivates us about death, leaving us overwhelmed but silently possessed of a feeling of sacredness or voidness, isn't the dead body as such. If we see (or see in our imaginations) the horror of death as an actuality—the cadaver plain and simple, and its decay—

we experience only disgust. The high-minded respect, calmness, even the gentle reverence with which we offer tribute, is related to artificial aspects. Hence the apparent serenity of a dead person whose jaw a couple of hours earlier was wrapped shut. It's the same with sensuality—a transposition is required in order for us to be attracted to nothingness. We're horrified by excretions, even insurmountably disgusted. We limit ourselves to being attracted to a condition wherein a transposition is possible—to being drawn to a nakedness that we can choose to see as immediately attractive for reasons of skin tone or formal purity. The obscenity of bodies derives from a disgust with excretion, put aside out of shame, while at the same time we ignore the formal ugliness of the organs. Obscenity is a zone of nothingness we have to cross—without which beauty lacks the suspended, risked aspect that brings about our damnation. Attractive, voluptuous nakedness finally triumphs when defilement causes us to risk ourselves (though in other cases, nakedness fails because it remains ugliness wholly at the level of defilement).

If I now bring in the notion of temptation (often independent of the idea of sin, since our resistance often is out of fear of unpleasant consequences), it's in order to note that in the interplay of the flesh, individual existences are obviously asserted as movement.

Temptation locates sexual misconduct as a confrontation with boredom. We aren't always prey to boredom, and life retains the possibility of numerous communications. But if that possibility fails, boredom then discloses the nothingness of self-enclosure. When separate existence stops communicating, it withers. It wastes away, (obscurely) feeling that *by itself it doesn't exist.* Unproductive and unattractive, such inner nothingness repels us. It brings about a fall into restless boredom, and boredom transfers the restlessness from inner nothingness to outer nothingness—or anguish.

In states of temptation, this transfer—in anguish—dwells endlessly on the nothingness with which a desire to communicate confronts us. If I contemplate the nothingness of obscenity independently of desire and so to speak on its own behalf, I only note the sensible, graspable sign of a limit at which being is confronted with lack. But in temptation, the outer nothingness appears as a reply to a yearning for communication.

The meaning and reality of this reply are easy to determine. I only communicate outside of me by letting go or being pushed to this outside. Still, outside of me, I don't exist. There's no doubt in my mind that to let go of existence inside me and to look for it outside is to take a chance on ruining or annihilating precisely whatever it is without which the outer existence wouldn't have appeared in the first place—the *self*—which is the precondition for there being a "mine." With temptation, if I can put it this way, we're crushed by twin pincers of nothingness. By not communicating, we're annihilated into the emptiness of an isolated life. By communicating we likewise risk being destroyed.

Of course defilement is the real issue, and defilement isn't death. Nonetheless, if under shameful conditions I give in—and so pay for a streetwalker—even if I don't die, I'm still ruined and fallen in my own judgment. Crude obscenity gnaws away at my existence, its excremental nature rubbing off on me—this nothingness carried by filth, this nothingness I should have expelled, this nothingness I should have distanced myself from—and I'm left defenseless and vulnerable, opening myself to it in an exhausting wound.

Clearly, ongoing resistance to temptation will accentuate this aspect of a life of the flesh. But the same element enters into all sensuality. Even weak communication requires a risk. It only takes place if individuals, leaning out over themselves, risk themselves under the threat of decline. This is why even the purest souls *aren't unaware* of the sinkholes of ordinary sensuality (Despite themselves, they can't exclude a familiarity with this). The purity to which they're attached signifies that even the tiniest, most negligible portion of ignominy is enough to catch hold of them. With extreme aversion, they guess what drains others. The long and the short of it is, we all get h——* for the same reasons.

*Bataille's euphemism, referring to "hard"—TRANS.

IV

It was right for the other, the preacher of the humble, to suffer and bear humankind's sins. As for me, I rejoice in great sin as in my great solace.

—*Zarathustra*, "On the Superman"

. . . the highest good and highest evil are the same.

—1885–86

INDIVIDUALS OR humans can only "communicate"—*live*—outside of themselves. And being under the necessity to "communicate," they're compelled to *will* evil and defilement, which, by risking the being within them, renders them mutually penetrable each to the other.

I once wrote (*Inner Experience*), "What you are relates to an activity that links the uncounted elements that compose you to an intense communication of these elements among themselves. These elements are contagions of energy, movement, and heat, or transfers of elements, and they constitute the inner life of all organic beings. Life is never situated at some specific point, but quickly moves from one point to another (or from multiple points to other points) like a current or sort of electrical stream . . ." And further on, "Your life is not limited to that incomprehensible inner stream; it also streams out from itself, incessantly opening to whatever flows out or rushes up to it. The ongoing whirling that composes you collides with similar whirlings, which form a vast figure driven by rhythmic restlessness. Now, for you to live signifies not just the flows and momentary dispositions of light that unite in you but the movements of heat or

25

light moving from one person to another, or from you to another person, or from another to you (even as you now read me, the contagion of my fever reaches you): words, books, monuments, symbols, laughter—all these represent just so many paths to that contagiousness, to those impulses . . ."

But these burning trajectories only replace isolated humanness if there's some consent, if not to annihilation, then to *risking* yourself and, in the same impulse, *risking* other people.

All "communication" participates in suicide, in crime.

Lethal horror goes with it, and disgust is its sign.

And in such a light, evil appears—as a life source!

By destroying the integrity of existence in myself and in others, I open myself to communion—I attain a moral summit.

And the summit isn't a *submission to* but a *willing* of evil. It is a voluntary pact with sin, crime, and evil. A pact made with a relentless fate that requires that while some live, others die.

V

And they believed in all that!
They called it moral!
Écrasez l'infame!

Have you understood? Dionysus facing the Crucified . . .

—Ecce Homo

To MAKE distinctions is simply impoverishment—even the least
holding back offends fate. Whatever, for *it*, is simply *excessiveness
harmful to excessivness itself*, for another person isn't so at all. For
someone else *positioned further on*. Is it true *nothing human is foreign to
me?* Gambling, risking, even the smallest bet—I open up the prospect of infinitely upping the ante.

Within that retreating prospect can be glimpsed a summit.

*As the highest point (or most intense degree) of life's attraction to itself that
life itself can define.*

As a kind of solar explosion, independent of consequences.

In what precedes I've presented evil as a means to use to "communicate."

I've stated: "without evil, human existence would be enclosed in
itself," or ". . . evil appears . . . as a life source!" Thus I suggested a
fictional relationship. By letting "communication" be seen as the
good of being, I identified "communication" precisely with the
being that it exceeds. Inasmuch as "communication," evil, or summit, are "the good of being," to be honest, they're reduced to the
slavishness they can't be surrendered to. The very notions of *good* or

27

being interpose a duration and concern that *essentially* are unknown to evil or summit. What is *substantially* rejected in evil is a concern with the time to come. It's precisely in this sense that longing for summit—*that our impulses toward evil—constitute all morality within us.* Morality in *itself* has no *value* (in the strong sense) except as it leads to going beyond being and rejecting concerns for a time to come.

Morality has value only when advising us to risk ourselves. Otherwise it's only a rule of interest, lacking any element of elation (the giddiness of the summit baptized by impoverishment under a servile and imperative name).

Juxtaposed with these propositions, the essence of "popular morality" is most clearly brought to the fore when dealing with sexual license.

To the extent human beings take it on themselves to give others a rule of life, they must make an appeal to merit, propose the good of being as an end that finds accomplishment in the time to come.

If my life is threatened for some comprehensible good—for instance, for the nation or a useful cause—my behavior is deserving and is popularly considered moral. And for the same reasons I'll kill and wreck havoc *in conformity to moral law.*

In another area, squandering resources through gambling and drinking is wrong: though it's right to improve the fate of the poor.

Blood sacrifice itself is execrated (a cruel waste). But the object of the greatest loathing is the freedom of the senses.

Sexual life considered in relation to these ends is almost entirely excess—a savage eruption toward an inaccessible summit— exuberance as essential opposition to concerns for the time to come. The nothingness of obscenity can't be subjected to anything. The fact that it's not a cancellation of existence but only a notion, and one resulting from contact, far from alleviates, and actually increases the disapproval generally felt. It is unrelated to value. It is not as if the erotic summit is something heroic attained *at the cost of* harsh sufferings. Clearly, the results bear no relation to the efforts. Only chance seems in charge here. Chance plays a role in wartime disorders—though effort and courage assign the appreciable part to merit. War's tragical aspects, in contrast with the laughable indecencies of love-making, have the effect of raising the tone of morality, which extols war (and economic profits) to the detriment of any sensual life. I am afraid that I still haven't clearly enough demonstrated the naïveté of a moral bias. The weightier argument stresses the benefit to family life, which is clearly injured by sensual excess. Constantly identified with the harshness of moral yearnings, concern for the integrity of beings is painfully demonstrated.

In popular opinion, the substantive aspect of moral action is its subordination to utility, and the impulses for a yearning to transcend being are related to the good of one's being. In this view, morality becomes simply a negation of morality. The result of this equivocation is to contrast the good of others with the good of the particular being that I am. In fact, this shift continues to identify a superficial contempt with the deep submission that acts on behalf of being. Evil is egotism—altruism good.

VI

Morality simply is weariness.

—1882–85

Rather than being a reply to ardent desires for the summit, morality is more likely a barrier opposing them. Exhaustion quickly results, and inordinate expenses of energy to which the desire to break down being's limit compels us no longer encourage the preservation of our being, that is, our good. Whether we are dealing with sensuality or crime, ruin is implied for both agent and victim.

I don't mean that sensuality and crime always, or even ordinarily, correspond to a desire for a summit. A feckless sensuality pursues its banal disorders through individuals who simply "let go." What could be more common? Isn't this whatever with instinctive aversion we call *pleasure*, isn't this essentially a subordination, effected on the part of more ponderous individuals, of certain joyful excesses to which those of a lighter nature seek access as a means to self-loss? A crime reported in the newspapers has little to do with the ambiguous attractions of sacrifice. The disorder introduced by such crimes isn't intended to be for itself, but to serve *interests* that, though illegal, aren't so different (taking the insidious viewpoint) from interests of the more elevated kind. All the same, the lacerated regions designated by vice and crime indicate a summit to which passions lead.

What were the supreme moments of primitive life when our longings were freely expressed? Celebrations (for which we still yearn) were times of sacrifice and orgy.

VII

The happiness we find in becoming is possible only by annihilating the reality of "existences" and lovely appearance, and through the pessimistic destruction of illusions: so, by annihilating even the loveliest appearances, Dionysian happiness attains its height.

—1885–86

IF, IN the light of the principles that I've presented, I now return to Christian ecstasy, I'm free to regard it as part of a single impulse that encompasses erotic and criminal transports.

More than any believer, Christian mystics crucify Jesus. The mystic's love requires God to risk himself, to shriek out his despair on the cross. The basic crime associated with the saints is erotic, related to the transports and tortured fevers that produce a burning love in the solitude of monasteries and convents.

Aspects of the extreme laceration evident in prayer at the foot of the cross can be compared to non-Christian mystical states. For both, sexual desire awakens ecstatic moments, and the object of the love that is this impulse inexorably becomes the individual's annihilation. Sometimes the nothingness connected to mystical states is the nothingness of the subject, sometimes the individual's nothingness considered within the world totality. The "night of anguish" theme is found in one form or other in Asian meditations.

Whatever the religious tradition from which mystical trance is derived, it exhausts itself by exceeding being. Taken at a fever pitch, the fire within relentlessly consumes whatever gives people and things their stable appearance—whatever gives them confidence,

31

whatever acts as a support. Little by little, desire lifts the mystic to such utter ruin and expenditure that the life of that person becomes more or less a solar brightness.

Clearly, however, whether we are dealing with yogis, Buddhists, or Christian monks, there is no reality to such ruins, to such perfections associated with desire. With them, crime or the annihilation of existence is a representation. Their general compromise with regard to morality can easily be shown. Real license was rejected from the arena of the possible as being fraught with unpleasant consequences: orgies or sacrifices, for instance. But since there remains the desire for a summit with which these acts are connected, and since beings are still under the necessity of "communicating" with their beyond, symbols (or fictions) have replaced reality. The sacrifice of the mass as representing the reality of the death of Jesus is simply a symbol of the infinite renewal of the Church. Meditational subjects have taken the place of real orgies, drunkenness, and flesh and blood—the latter becoming objects of disapproval. In this way there still remained a summit connected with desire, while the various violations of existence related to that summit no longer were compromising, since now they had become mental representations.

VIII

And as for decadence, *the image of this in many ways is people who do not die prematurely; from their experience, they know the instincts that this implies; during nearly* half their lives *human beings are decadent.*

—1888

Substitution of spiritual summits for immediate ones, however, won't take place if we don't admit the primacy of the future over the present and if we don't draw the consequences of the inevitable decline that follows the summit. Spiritual summits are a negation of what might be given as a summit morality. And they fall into the category 'the morality of the decline.'

THE SHIFT to spiritual forms requires one main condition, since a pretext would be necessary before rejecting sensuality. If I suppressed consideration of the time to come, I wouldn't be in a position to resist temptation. I must helplessly give in to the slightest impulse. Temptation isn't even a notion that can occur to me: from then on temptation is ruled out, and I'm easy prey for desires that now can be thwarted only through outward difficulties. To be honest, this blessed openness isn't humanly imaginable. Human nature can't *as such* reject worries about the future, and the states in which such preoccupations aren't applicable are either above humanness or below it.

Whatever the case, we escape a giddying sensuality only by representing for ourselves some good situated in a future time, a future that sensuality would destroy and that we have to keep from it. So we can reach the summit beyond the fever of the senses only provided

33

we set up a subsequent goal. Or, if you like (a clearer, more serious consideration), we reach a nonsensual, nonimmediate summit only by referring to a necessarily higher end. And this end isn't simply located above sensuality (which it brings to a halt); it also must be situated *above the spiritual summit.* Beyond sensuality, beyond the reply to desire, we are in fact in the realm of the good—which is the realm of the primacy of the future against the present, the area of being's preservation, contrasted with its glorious loss.

Another way of saying this: resistance to temptation implies abandoning the summit morality, belonging, as this resistance does, to the morality of decline. When we feel our strength ebbing and we decline, we condemn excesses of expenditure in the name of some higher good. As long as youthful excitement impels us, we consent to dangerous squandering, boldly taking the risks that present themselves. But as soon as our strength begins to ebb or we start to perceive the limits of this strength (*when we start to decline*), we're preoccupied with gaining and accumulating goods of all kinds, acquiring wealth, since we're thinking of the difficulties to come. We act. And the end of action and efforts can only be the acquisition of strength. Now, to the extent that a spiritual summit—which opposes sensuality and pits itself against it—becomes revealed in an unfolding action, it's associated with efforts that desire to gain some good. Such a summit no longer comes within the rubric of a *summit morality*, and a *decline morality* prompts it not so much to desire as to make efforts.

IX

I can't recall efforts, there's no trace of struggle in my life, and I'm the opposite of heroic natures. My experience knows nothing at all about what it means to "will" a thing or work at it ambitiously or relate to some "goal" or realization of desire.

—Ecce Homo

So that ordinarily, mystical states are conditioned by a search for salvation.

IT APPEARS that the summit's link between a mystical state and impoverished existence, with fear and greed expressed as values of decline, is in a sense superficial and very likely to be deeply fallacious. This doesn't make it any less what is the case. Solitary ascetics pursue an end whose means is ecstasy—and ascetics *work* for their salvation like merchants buying and selling with profit in mind or like workers sweating for their wages. If workers or merchants had wealth for the asking, without worries about a future, without fearing death or destruction, they'd leave their workplace or business without further ado and seek out whatever dangerous pleasures presented themselves. As for ascetics: by falling into common human misery, they become possessed by a possibility of undertaking the lengthy work of deliverance.

Ascetic practices are *human* precisely insofar as they aren't much different from surveying work. To be sure, the greatest difficulty in the end is to take cognizance of that limitation. Without the bait of salvation (or something like it), who could ever discover the mystical way? People must have agreed among themselves (or among others),

35

that this or that is advisable in view of this or that result, this or that
gain. Without these crude artifices they wouldn't have committed
themselves to the behavior that marks out decline (the infinite sadness, the ridiculous seriousness required by effort!). Isn't it obvious?
As soon as I say—oh why give a damn about some future!—then and
there I break into infinite laughter. At the same moment, though,
I've lost the reason to make *efforts*.

X

What you see is the birth of a hybrid species, the artist— removed from crime through weakness of will and fear of society, though not yet ready for the insane asylum, and oddly extending his antennae in both directions.

—1888

We have to go further.
To articulate such a critique is already to decline.
The fact of "speaking" of a summit morality itself belongs to a decline of morality.

HAVING SAID good-bye to worries about the future with a blasphemous oath—I lose all reason for existing, in fact, all reason, period.

I lose the possibility of *speaking*.

Especially *speaking* as I am now of summit morality is something utterly ridiculous!

Out of what reason and to what end, going beyond the summit itself, would I want to explain such a morality?

And to begin with, how to structure the explanation?

To me, to structure and explain the summit morality assumes the decline, since it assumes accepting moral rules relating to fear. Frankly put, the summit, when suggested as an end, is not the summit, since I'm reducing it to the search for advantage *when speaking of it*. To construe utter dissipation as the moral summit is to completely change its nature. Specifically: in such dissipation I'm thus depriving myself of the power of reaching the summit.

The only possible way for dissipation to reach the summit is by not intending it. The ultimate moment of the senses requires real innocence and absence of moral pretensions and, as a result, even a feeling of evil.

XI

Like Kafka's castle, in the final analysis the summit is simply whatever is inaccessible. It slips away from us, at least until we stop being human, that is, until we stop speaking.

The summit can, though, be opposed to decline as evil to good.

The summit isn't "what we ought to reach"; nor is decline "what ought to be done away with."

Just as in the last analysis the summit is simply inaccessible, from the start, decline is inevitable.

PUTTING ASIDE popular confusions, though, I haven't done away with the necessity for a summit (I haven't done away with the desire for it). Admitting its inaccessible nature (I approach it only by not setting out for it), I'm not on that score compelled to accept the undisputed sovereignty of the decline (speaking commits me to this stance). I can't deny the inevitability of decline. The summit itself indicates it. If the summit isn't death, the necessity of descent follows thereafter. Essentially, the summit is where life is pushed to an impossible limit. I reach it, in the faint way that I do, only by recklessly expending my strength. I won't again possess a strength to waste unless, through work, I can gain back the strength lost. What am I moreover? Inscribed in a human context, I can't dispossess myself of my will to act. The possibility of giving up work forever and in some way pushing myself definitively to some goal, which in the long run is illusory: This isn't conceivable. Let's even suppose (in an ideal way) that I'm considering the Caesarean option of suicide. This albeit attractive possibility arises for me as an endeavor causing me to place concerns for the future over those for the present. But I can't give up the summit! I protest (intending to put lucid, dispassionate ardor into such protests) against anything that asks of us that we stifle desire. Though I can only contentedly resign myself to the fate compelling me to work: I'd never dream of *doing away with* moral *rules*, since they spring from inevitable decline. We are always declining, and ruinous desire returns again only as strength is restored. Because powerlessness in us requires recognition, and because we don't have unlimited strength, why not acknowledge such a necessity, giving in to it even as we deny it? We're no match for the empty sky that infinitely assaults and annihilates us down to the last human being. I can only morosely say, of the necessity to which I submit, that it *humanizes* me by giving me undeniable dominion over things. I have the option, however, of not regarding it as a sign of weakness.

XII

And again and again the human species claimed, "We definitely don't have the right to just laugh at anything!" And the most prescient philosophers added, "Not just laughter and joyful prudence, but tragedy and sublime folly too, are among the means and necessities of preserving the species."—This is consistent!—it follows!

—*Gay Science*

MORAL AMBIGUITIES constitute a fairly stable system of equilibrium regarded from the standpoint of existence generally. But we can never completely go back to them. Who would deny that self-sacrifice has a place in the scheme of things? Should we be surprised if that involves compromise with well-understood common interests? Still, the existence of morality and the confusion generated by it extend my investigation far beyond such an immediate outlook. In the lengthy and preceding considerations, I don't know if I've made it sufficiently clear how lacerating this last investigation has been. I'll now develop a viewpoint that, though external to the simple questions I wanted to introduce, nonetheless brings out their implications.

As long as the excessive impulses to which desire leads can be linked to useful actions or considered to be such (useful, that is, for individuals in decline, who are reduced to the necessity of accumulating strength), there was a way to fulfill the desire for a summit. Thus people of other times made sacrifices, even indulged in orgies while attributing to sacrifice and orgy an efficacy of action that would act to benefit the clan or the state. Any violation of others, like war, possesses a beneficial value so long as it finds success—and rightly so. Beyond narrow, visibly heavy-handed, egotistical political benefits, and despite the possibilities of individual self-sacrifice, the inequities in the division of state wealth (arising from disorder) made people seek some good that would accord with the feeling for justice. Beyond the egotistical state good, salvation (or the concern for personal salvation after death) became the motivation for action and, as well, the means to link action to an ascent to the summit and to a surpassing of self. In a general way, personal salvation allowed escape from the lacerations breaking down society. Injustice became tolerable. It allowed the possibility of appeal, and people even began joining together in their effort to fight the results of injustice. Beyond the specific goods considered to be so many motives for action by the state and then the Church (the Church in turn becoming the analog for the state, so that during the Crusades people will die for it), the possibility of radically abolishing the obstacle created by unequal conditions defined a sort of beneficial action and motivated the sacrifice of lives. So throughout history—and in the process of making history—there developed *reasons* to proceed to the summit and risk ourselves. The difficulty beyond this is to proceed to the summit without motivation and without pretext. As I said, to speak of the summit is to put ourselves in a position of instability. *We only discover it by speaking of something else.*

To put it another way. Because all risk, ascent, and sacrifice, like sensual excess, is loss of strength or expenditure, we have to motivate expenditures each time with promises of advantage, whether illusory or not.

Envisaged in a general economy, this situation seems strange.

I can imagine some kind of historical situation in which all possibilities of action are put on hold, kept in reserve, like the agèd when they live beyond life's limits, abrogating all their further hopes and plans beyond limits already attained. Revolutionary action would found classless society, beyond which further historical action wouldn't arise. Or so I assume in any event. Still, I have to make an observation. In a general way, apparently, humanly speaking, the sum of energy produced is always greater than the sum necessary for its production. Hence the continuous and overly full churning out of energy, leading us endlessly to some summit, constituting a *baleful* element that (largely pointlessly) we attempt to expend for a common *good*. Governed by concerns with the good and the primacy of the future, the mind considers it repugnant to contemplate squanderings that might be defined as *guilty*, or useless, or even harmful. Now, since the motivations for action are missing which till now have been pretexts for infinite squandering, it seems humanity is discovering possibilities for rest and for recovery . . . But what then will we do with the excess energies that fall to our lot? . . .

I've tried insidiously to suggest the external ramifications that my question might have. In all honesty, I have to admit that, as it stands—on the level of economic calculation—the question loses in sharpness what it has gained in amplitude. The reality is, the question has changed. The more interest came to be factored in, the more expenditure had to depend on it. That is an obvious dead-end, since in the long run we can't continue spending to gain—and as I've said, *the sum of energy produced is always greater* . . .

XIII

Now I'LL articulate some of the questions implicit in the account I gave.

Is there a moral goal that I can reach beyond being?

To which I have already answered, in any event, that I wouldn't be able to go searching for it—or talking about it.

I live, and in me is life (language). Now, the language that is in me can't give up having a moral goal . . . All it can do is suggest that if I follow the slopes of decline, I'll never arrive at that goal.

And this said, I continue to live.

I'll add (speaking in my name), I can't find a *good* to substitute for the goal eluding me.

I no longer know of any reason—outside me—to sacrifice either myself or the small quantity of strength I have.

I live, vulnerable to laughter on one hand (leaving me cheerful), and sexual stimulation on the other (leaving me anxious).

Mystical states are available to me, if that is what I want.

Maintaining my distance from beliefs, deprived of hopes, nothing compels me to enter these states.

I feel removed from the notion of making efforts to attain them.

Making my inner experience a project: doesn't that result in a remoteness, on my part, from the summit that might have been?

With those who have motives and reasons, I don't feel as if I'm missing anything, so I'm not envious. Just the opposite. Since I encourage them to share my fate. My mistrust of motivations and fragility, are, I think, propitious. The greatest difficulty in my situation is my luck. I'm intoxicated by it.

But exploding inside me, despite everything, is a question: WHAT CAN A CLEAR-SIGHTED PERSON DO IN THIS WORLD, HAVING INCONTROVERTIBLE DEMANDS WITHIN?

XIV

*You are not eagles. Which is why you haven't comprehended
the blissfulness of terror in your minds. Not being birds, how
do you propose to nest on an abyss?*

—*Zarathustra*, "On Illustrious Sages"

RAISING THE question like this, I said what I had to say—I have no
answers. In working this out, I put aside desires for *autonomy* and
longings for *freedom*—though these longings seem a human passion
and certainly are mine. I'm thinking less of the freedom wrested by
individuals from public powers and more of the human autonomy at
the heart of a hostile, silent nature. True, the bias that depends on
given facts as little as possible implies indifference to the time to
come. But it also opposes the satisfying of desire. Still, I regard the
summit about which I've spoken as freedom.

In an effort to clarify this connection, let me take a detour.

No matter how much care we exercise, our thinking is exhausted
without ever embracing the possibilities of totality. At each moment
we feel an enigmatic night, in its infinitely great depths, stealing
away with the very object of our reflections. The smallest thought
should be worked out infinitely. When the desire to grasp the truth
takes hold of me—and here I mean the desire to know and to reach
out to the light—I am gripped by feelings of desperation. And
immediately, I am (forever) lost in a world in which I have no more
power than a small child (except there aren't any adults helping
me). In all truthfulness, the more I attempt to reflect on this, the
more the outcome I anticipate fails to turn out to be a situation
where light is produced, and becomes one where it is extinguished.

And once again I am in the night like a sick child, like someone dying.

If you sincerely longed for the truth, you wouldn't share this indifference of mine. Your job each time would be to exhaust the infinite working out of possibilities. I'm not against attempts like these which demand youthful boldness. Still, if, when I have to act, it's not required of me that I consider objects in the infinite working out of their aspects (I manipulate them—the efficaciousness of my movements corresponding to the value of my ideas), then similarly, when I have to question, naturally I have to go the limit, though "going the limit" means "doing my best"—while if I desired Truth, I'd be called upon to satisfy absolute demands. The reason for this is that while I can't get along without acting or questioning, on the other hand I am able to *live*—to act or question—without knowing. Perhaps the desire to know has just one meaning—as a motivation for the desire to question. Naturally, knowing is necessary for human autonomy procured through action by which the world is transformed. But beyond any conditions for *doing or making*, knowledge finally appears as a deception in relation to the questioning that impels it. When questioning fails, we laugh. Ecstatic raptures and the ardors of love are so many questions—without answers—to which nature and our nature are subjected. If I had the ability to respond to moral questions like the ones I've indicated, to be honest, I'd be putting the summit at a distance from myself. By leaving open such questions in me like a wound, I keep my chance, I keep luck, and I maintain a possible access to these questions.

If I speak as I do now, it's basically to recline like a sick man or, to be precise, to recline and die. But this doesn't mean that I'm not calling for the doctor. I have to apologize for excess irony. The truth is, I never wanted to make fun of anyone. I only wanted to make fun of the *world*—meaning the incomprehensible nature from which I arose. We're not used to taking this into account if we reflect and speak—but death will interrupt us. I won't always be required to continue the servile search for the true. Every question will remain finally unanswered. And I'll slip off in such a way so as to impose silence. If others begin the job anew, they won't get any further—and death will cut off their words just as it does mine. Will human existence ever have a more authentic autonomy? Speaking like this, it seems to me that existence breathes the free air of the summit.

Existence can't, at one and the same time, be both autonomous and viable.

PART III

Diary
February—
August 1944

February–April 1944

_____

The new feeling of power: the mystical state. And the clearest and most daring rationalism acts as a path to it.

—1884

I

. . . no matter how it happened, each time "the hero" strode across the stage, something new was attained, a terrible reverse of laughter, a profound emotion for many in their thought: "Yes, life is worth living! Yes, I'm worthy of life!"— Life, you and me, all of us just as we are, we became interesting to ourselves. We cannot deny that in the long run laughter, reason, and nature ended up becoming masters of each of the great masters of teleology: Brief-tenured tragedy finally has always returned to the eternal comedy of existence. And the sea "with its countless smiles"—to speak with Aeschylus—with its waves, will finally cover the greatest of our tragedies. . . .

—*Gay Science*

If you neglect to note a casual attitude that dismisses the most deeply-rooted problems, making a game of everything (especially misfortune and suffering), cloaking success under the mantle of depression, I am, if you insist, a sorry person . . . What I've done, however, is simply to associate lovemaking and its outrageous pleasures with integral disrespect, with the radical rejection of whatever constrains inner freedom.

My desire today is focused on a point. This object without objective truth is the most awesome I can imagine—and I compare it to a smile or to the transparency of the beloved. No embrace can attain this transparency (it's specifically whatever flees at the instant of possession). It's lacerated by a desire that I've seen beyond any

53

desirable presence, and it's a point whose sweetness and gentleness is given in despair.

This is the object I recognized, that I awaited so long! It's out of feelings of response that we recognize the beloved: the beloved is someone expected, someone filling some emptiness (without him or her a universe turns incomprehensible). Still, the woman I hold in my arms eludes me, and vainly with this embrace do I attempt to recover feelings that, in reply to expectation, had turned to certainties. Only absence, *through feelings of lack*, continues to attain this beloved.

Whatever I may have said before (I'm unclear on this as I write): it now seems to me that Proust, speaking of remembering, gave an accurate description of this object.

Now this object, perceived in ecstasy, though in calm clarity, in a way differs from the beloved. This object is what, in the beloved, leaves an intimate, incomprehensible, lacerating impression of déjà vu.

As to the odd tale known as *Remembrance of Things Past*—in which life is slowly collapsed and dissolved in inanity (inability to grasp), though grasping the ocellar points wherein it is resolved—it seems to me that this story has the inner truth of a sob.

Sobbing signifies a break-down in communication. When communication—the sweetness of intimate communication—is cut off by death, separation, or misunderstanding, I feel a less familiar sweetness, a sweetness that's a sobbing within me—and this is laceration. Still, the sweetness of sobbing is significantly different from the previous sort of sweetness. In any established communication, habit suppresses attraction. In sobbing, the attraction is similar to the spark caused by a plug being pulled out from a wall socket. Because the communication has broken off (and precisely because of this) we possess it in a tragic mode when we weep.

Proust believed his memory retained that which just the same escaped. Memory completely reveals what presence made off with, though perhaps only for a time. In a sense it's true to say human sobbing gives a faint foretaste of eternity.

How much I admire the undoubtedly conscious cunning with which the final book *The Past Recaptured* reneges on what others located in the infinite limits of a teacup. If with André Breton you speak of "a dazzling, sightless interior life . . . whose soul is as much ice as fire," there remains in the flash thereby elicited a great and transcendent "something" that, in the depths of our human souls, maintains a relationship of superiority, going from men to God. The uneasiness thus produced is probably inevitable. We only let go of ourselves when experiencing laceration. I don't want to flee transcendent moments (moments that *The Past Recaptured* disguises). It seems to me, however, that human transcendence is by nature negative. I lack the power of putting any object *above* me, whether to apprehend it or let it lacerate me, except for nothingness, which doesn't exist. And as regards a particular portion of being—what confers on it the impression of transcendence is our perception of it as mediated by nothingness. Only through lacerating nothingness do we arrive at the beyond of the specific existence that we are. We're overwhelmed and crushed by nothingness—tempted to attribute powers of domination to whatever we intuit as being in the shadows. As a result, and in one of our most human moments, we transfer to the human scale objects we consider resistant to collapse. These objects aren't deflated, but a development of sovereign simplicity reveals their inner nature.

To destroy transcendence, there has to be laughter. Just as children left alone with the frightening beyond that is in themselves are suddenly aware of their mother's playful gentleness and answer her with laughter: in much the same way, as my relaxed innocence perceives trembling as play, I break out laughing, illuminated, laughing all the more from having trembled.

It's hard to speak of this strange and particularly felicitous laughter. It supports the nothingness that once was used as the infinite pedestal for the tiny figure of God (the image of humanness). At each moment my fear snatches me out of myself and out of my minor worries—and leaves me to nothingness.

In this nothingness in which I exist (questioning to the point of nausea, so that every answer I get seems to push the void that much further out, doubling the questioning) I can make out nothing—and God as an answer is as empty as the "nature" found in crude materialism. Nonetheless I can't disavow the possibilities given to those who shape God into an image. Because, humanly, the experience of him exists, and we are familiar with his stories.

The time came when the audacity (or if you will, indifference) that represented me asked, "Couldn't you too have a demented experience like that and then laugh at it?" And I answered, "That can't be: I don't have *faith*!" In the silence in which I found myself crazily open to every possibility, I remained perched on the void—and everything seemed equally ridiculous, hideous, and *possible* to me . . . At that instant I passed beyond. Then and there I recognized God.

Being provoked by infinite laughter didn't make this any more comfortable.

I threw myself at the feet of that old ghost.

Ordinarily we have but a paltry notion of such majesty: a disclosure of it was made to me in full measure.

The shadows became an infinite black beard issuing from earth's depths and gory blood.

I laughed.

It was infinitely more ponderous.

But my lightness proceeded to deal with it effortlessly—giving back to nothingness what is simply nothingness.

Outside freedom, outside laughter itself, there's nothing I laugh at more divinely than God.

II

We want to inherit *all ancient morality, not start again. All of our activity is only morality turning against the older forms.*

—1880–84

I THOUGHT friends of mine had confused their concern for a desirable value with contempt for the low. Value (or the object of moral longing) isn't something that can be attained. No one is to be seen as unworthy of love. Speaking as a malcontent, I'm instinctively sympathetic. I no longer see an ideal when confronted with decline. It is a sad thing and a sorry sight to see the collapse of most people, their heroic ardors and moral determination turning into stifling narrowness. Often their stubborn inflexibility indicates the fact of wavering (simpering Christians, bombastic activists). What I like is only lovemaking, desire . . .

In categorical condemnations, when we call someone a "slime" while overlooking the "sliminess" we don't want to see in ourselves, the very harshness of insensitivity for which we censured him is intensified by our own meanness. It's the same with the police—society approximates procedures similar to those it condemns.

Complicity, first in the crime itself and then in ignoring it, unites humanity in the most intimate way possible.

Union with another fuels unending hostility. In the excesses of lovemaking, I'm driven not only to kill but to keep from fainting and falling down at the prospect. If I could, I'd fall shrieking in despair.

But rejecting despair, and continuing to live happily and playfully (without a motivation for this), I love in a tougher, truer way, to the extent that life is worth loving.

The chance belonging to lovers is lovers' luck: the evil (disequilibrium) to which they're driven in lovemaking compels them. They're endlessly sentenced to destroy the harmony between themselves and at night to begin combat. These maneuvers and wounds are the cost of their uniting.

Moral value is the object of our desire and what we die for. It's not always an "object" (with a definite existence). Desire often is associated with an indefinite presence. God and a woman who is loved are parallel. Contrasted to them would be nothingness and woman's nakedness (irrespective of any particular woman).

Logically, indefiniteness has a negative sign.

I really hate complacent laughter, the cliquish humor of the so-called witty.

Nothing is less characteristic of me than bitter laughter.

I laugh innocently and divinely. I don't laugh when I'm depressed—and when I do laugh, I'm having fun.

Embarrassed at having laughed (with friends) at the crimes of Dr. Petiot.* The laughter that in all likelihood has the summit as its object arises from our not being conscious of it. Like the friends I mentioned, I'm moved from nameless horror to mindless laughter. Beyond laughter there is death, desire (love), fainting, and the ecstasy associated with horror, a horror transfigured. In this beyond, laughter stops, though I retain my awareness of it. Attempts to continue with this and pry open the beyond would make laughter something "intended" and so ring false from lack of simplicity. Spontaneous and unrestrained laughter opens on the worst, pre-

* A serial murderer famous in Bataille's day. Akin to Sweeney Todd, he'd use a "periscope" from the adjoining room to watch patients die horrible deaths, then melt them down—TRANS.

serving in the worst (death) a weightless feeling of wonder (at the
devil God, at blasphemies, or transcendence! The universe is humble, my laughter is its innocence).

Laughter blesses where God curses. Unlike God, humanity isn't
condemned to condemn. Laughter can be filled with wonder if that is
what humanity wants it to be—it can be light and it *itself* can bless.
What if I laugh at myself?

Petiot used to say to his patients (according to Q):

"I think you're anemic. You need calcium."

He'd make them appointments for calcium treatments on rue
Lesueur.

And what if I said that the periscope used on rue Lesueur is the
summit?

Horror and disgust would make me feel like throwing up.

Can nearness to the summit be discerned in wrenching horror and
disgust?

Do only coarse and primitive types give in to their compulsions to
use the periscope?

From the theological viewpoint the analogue of the periscope is
Calvary. With both, *sinners get off on* the results of crimes that they
committed. For believers, just the imagery is enough. However, this
crime of the crucifixion is their crime, and they associate repentance
with action. For them perversion ought to be equated with shifting
consciousness, involuntary dissimulation of action, lack of manliness,
flight.

Not long before the war, I dreamed of being struck by lightning.
Inside me I felt a wrenching and a great terror. At the same time there
was a sense of something wonderful and transfiguring: I was dying.

Today I feel the same surge within me. If I wanted things to go my
way or needed moral assurances, I would feel this joy was wrongheaded. But the opposite is true. And my intoxication comes from a
not willing, from not having any assurances. There is the feeling of

freedom within me. And if this surge is unto death, the pleasure doesn't come from being freed from life, but contrariwise from being relieved of the worries that erode life (worries that link it with definite conceptions). Practically nothing—only nothingness—intoxicates me. This intoxication has as its condition that I laugh, principally, at myself.

III

THE GREATEST, most certain love doesn't prevent you from being the butt of infinite laughter. Such love can be likened to an utterly demented music, to ecstatic lucidity.

My obsessive need to make love opens on death like a window on a courtyard.

To the extent that lovemaking calls up death (like the comical ripping apart of a painted stage set), it has the power to pull the clouds from the sky. It's utterly easy! With the clouds pulled away, I see: as if the world's nonmeaning were in complicity with me, its foundation appears free and empty.

In what way would the beloved differ from this empty freedom— or from the infinite transparency of something freed at last from a burden of meaning?

In this annihilating freedom, giddiness is transformed into rapturous calm.

The strength that lovers have (or their movement toward freedom), their violence, their fears, their ever-present expectation of making love, their skittish intolerance, these all contribute to dissolving them into a void.

The void frees me from what attaches me. In the void there is nowhere to stop. Creating the void ahead of me, I immediately sense the beloved there—where there is nothing. What was I desperately in love with? A glimpse, an open door.

A sudden impulse and an irrepressible need—these annihilate the heaviness of the world.

IV

And how many new ideals are still possible when you think about it! Here's one: a minor one, occurring to me every five weeks or so in the course of wild, solitary walks, during serene moments of almost criminal happiness. To live life among fragile and absurd things; to be unfamiliar with the real! Half artist, half bird or metaphysician. Not to say yes or no to reality except maybe occasionally, testing it with a foot, like a good dancer; to always feel kissed with a ray of sunlight and happiness; to be filled with joy and always feel stimulated, even by affliction, since affliction upholds *the happy man, and to see even in the most sacred things something comical. Such of course is the ideal of weighty minds, heavy with the weight of tons on them—quintessential souls of heaviness.*

—March–July 1888

W OKE UP this morning in a good mood.

I'm as blasphemous and cheerful as possible.

I don't want to continue speaking of *inner* (or mystical) experience right now but *impalement.* You might also say Zen. There's a kind of lightheartedness in giving names to specific sorts of experience, as if to flowers.

Impalement differs from Zen. Somewhat. It's a ridiculous way of behaving. In addition, it is difficult to define, like Zen.

I was showing off—while on this subject—when I said "torment." (I must have said it with enough weightiness, truthfulness, and passion to cause some misunderstanding: but the misunderstanding was necessary, just as the joke had to turn out to be true.)

Today I'm insisting by saying "impalement."

From the outset, teaching impalement as a practice is ludicrous. It implies the conviction that "I am not going to teach impalement." However I teach . . .

for a victim, impalement is the inaccessible summit. And isn't that the fundamental truth?

A possibility of anemic jokes turns my stomach—and they won't be lacking on the subject of impalement and Proust.

As soon as Proust's teacup is taken for what it is—God's fall (the fall of transcendence) into the ridiculous (into immediacy and immanence)—that teacup becomes impalement.

The summit's double nature (horror and delight, anguish and ecstasy) is depicted and brought out in stark contrasts in the two volumes of *Time Recaptured*. On one hand are the horrors of a squalid hotel. On the other, moments of bliss.

The differing moments of bliss:

—the diffuse impersonal and objectless joy of yoga;

—lacerating raptures, trances that inhibit breath,

—and again, more of the emptiness of night; which correspond to the untroubled transparence of *theopathic* states.

In these incomprehensibly transparent states, the mind remains inert and intensely lucid, free. The universe easily passes through the mind. The object is imposed on it in a "psychologically incomprehensible feeling of something that was here before, déjà vu."

As far as I'm concerned, "déjà vu" (a feeling of being penetrable from every direction, but also incomprehensibility) defines the theopathic state.

The traces of divine obtrusiveness now vanish. How could it be otherwise?

For the mystic (the believer), clearly, God evaporates, the mystic now *being* God.

At times it was entertaining to think I was God.

With theopathy it is different. Only this state takes comedy to an extreme limit, since it is infinite evaporation, effortless freedom, the reduction of everything to a movement of collapse.

To give expression to my feelings regarding the state indicated by the word I coined ("impalement"), I am writing the following few lines that ought to be regarded as the subject of meditation:

> *I call forth*
> *an object of allurement,*
> *sparkling, weightless*
> *flame,*
> *consuming,*
> *annihilating itself*
> *and so revealing the void,*
> *the identity of allurement*
> *intoxication*
> *and void.*
>
> *I call forth*
> *the void*
> *identical with flame,*
> *the cancellation of the object*
> *disclosing*
> *intoxicating*
> *illuminating*
> *flame.*

No practice can take you to the goal . . .

In every instance, I think, only suffering (devastating, exhausting your existence) opens such deep-seated wounds.

Such a condition of immanence defines blasphemy.

Perfect blasphemy negates nothingness (negates the power in nothingness). Nothing retains any hold on me, neither transcendence nor time to come (waiting no longer exists).

Not to speak about God is to be afraid of him, is to still feel uncomfortable about him (about his image or place in the interconnections of reality and language . . .), is to put off till later the examination of the emptiness he represents, put off shattering it with laughter.

To laugh at God, before whom multitudes trembled, requires simplicity, it needs the guileless rancor of children. Awkwardness and sickness are ruled out.

Impalement is laughter, but laughter so sharp it vanishes into thin air. Once you bore through immensity to the other side, the tiniest muscle's twitching, far from taking transparence to infinity, instead shatters it . . . Even the barely discernible smile on a Buddha would turn out awkward and heavy (a boring insistence on what's personal). Only an insistence on the leap, and a nimble lightness (the essence of autonomy and freedom), give laughter its limitless dominion.

Likewise the transparence of two individuals is disturbed by their carnal commingling.
I speak, obviously, of acute states.
The ordinary state of affairs is that I burst into laughter and I . . .

I've been called "God's widower" and "the grieving widower" . . .
This makes me laugh. The word flows and flows from my pen so that there is an inclination to think of this laughter as forced.
At one and the same time I'm entertained and depressed by that misunderstanding.
My laughter is lighthearted.
I've said that at the age of twenty a tide of laughter swept me away . . . I felt I was dancing in light. At the same time I surrendered to the joys of free sensuality.

Seldom does the world so satisfyingly laugh at someone who returns the laughter.

I remember confiding then (as we got to the marketplace) that the Siena cathedral made me laugh.

"You're crazy," they exclaimed. "How could a person laugh at beauty?!"

Nothing convinced them.

But I had laughed—boyishly happy on the square outside, looking at up the cathedral that under the July sky dazzled me.

I laughed at my pleasure in living and my Italianate sensuality—the softest, most graceful I know of. And I laughed to discover how much fun life had with Christianity in this sun-blessed spot, changing the anemic monk to the princess of *A Thousand and One Nights*.

Surrounded by pink and black-and-white palaces, Siena cathedral is an immense, multicolored golden cake in dubious taste.

V

W HEN ALL is said and done, I have more than one face. I don't know which is laughing at which.

Love is so excessive a feeling that I prop my head up in my hands. Arising from the passions, this realm of dreams isn't fundamentally a domain of lies. In the end the face is dispersed. In the place where the fabric of things rips open—in the lacerating rip—nothing remains but a person introduced into the fabric's texture.

Layers of dead leaves aren't steps ascending to a throne, and tugboat hoots disperse illusions of enchantment.

Though still, what would correspond to the magnificence of the world if no one spoke to us and communicated a (no doubt indecipherable) message: "As to this fate that befalls you, this fate you consider yours (the fate of the human being you are) or that you consider the destiny of existence generally (of the immensity you form part of), nothing allows you to reduce it to the poverty of things that remain only what they are. On the contrary, whenever a casual lie happens, or whenever something is transfigured, don't you hear an appeal which must be answered? You can't claim you wished for the journey, only that you are it. And who would challenge the utter distance, the extremity, the desirability of the way? Desirability?! Am I the measure of mysteries? If, perceiving me, you hadn't chosen an unreachable goal, you wouldn't even have approached the mystery!"

Of course night falls, but only to exasperate this desire.

I hate lies (poetic nonsense). But the desire within us has never lied. There's a sickness in desire that often makes us perceive some gap between the object imagined and the real object. It's true, the beloved individual differs from the conception I have of that individual. What's worse: to identify the real with the object of desire, it seems, presupposes extraordinary luck.

Contrary to which is the obvious splendor of a universe that reverses the idea we have of this chance. *If nothing in us veils the celestial glories, we are worthy of infinite love.* The beloved doesn't emerge from prosaic reality like a miracle from a series of defined facts. The chance transfiguring this beloved is only the absence of unhappiness. The universe acting within us denies itself in commonly occurring unhappiness (a dreary existence), but affirms itself with the chosen few.

Compared to the person I love, the universe seems poor and empty. This universe isn't "risked" since it's not "perishable."

But the beloved is the "beloved" for only a single person.

Carnal love, because not "sheltered from thieves" or vicissitudes, is greater than divine love.

It "risks" me and the one I love.

God by definition isn't risked.

However far the lovers of God go with their passion, they conceive of it as outside the play of risk, as beyond grace (in the happiness of the elect).

And it's true of course that a woman's lover can't give up (he's compelled to abolish tormenting absence) till at last he has her beneath his roof in his possession. The truth is that, for the most part, love is extinguished in attempts to elude its nature: which has to risk love again and again . . .

Is there anyone who can't comprehend the fact that happiness is the most demanding test of all for lovers? All the same, voluntarily renouncing it would be an artifice, would make love overly sophisticated, something intended, cunning, contrived (I think of lovers as willfully maintaining their difficult conditions). There remains, however small it be, a chance of going beyond, of exhausting happiness.

Chance, in French, has the same origin (*cadentia* in Latin) as *échéance* ("deadline"). Chance *échoit*, that is, it turns out to be the case. Or it just falls, *tombe* (like good luck or bad, originally). It is the randomness of dice as they fall.

Hence the whimsical idea that I am suggesting Hyperchristianity!

In that popular notion, it isn't humanity that falls and becomes separated from God—though God himself does (or to put it differently, the totality).

God here does not involve "less than his idea implies." In fact the opposite, more. But the "more" is cancelled out insofar as it is God—because God's essence is to be continuously "risked," or be "put into risk situations." In the end humankind remains alone.

To put this in a joking way—humankind is *generalized incarnation*!

Still, in the fall of universality into humankind, certain obnoxious pretenses at risk taking, such as with Jesus, no longer apply. (God only seems to relinquish Jesus). The surrender involved in risk taking is total.

What I love in the person I love—to the point of wanting to die from this love—isn't some individuated existence but the universal aspect of that person. Although this aspect is what risks itself, risks me.

At the popular level of these ideas, God himself is an individual and not a totality (God isn't me), although risk taking isn't applicable to the animals (they are by themselves).

How ponderous and grandiloquent that being is—compared to *beings that fall* (into the "teacup") of a human being.

Ponderousness is the price paid by impatience, by a search for security.

To speak about the absolute: an ignoble phrase, an inhuman term! Something you would imagine ghosts longing for.

I don't intend to make a deity out of anyone. And I laugh when God falls from banality into the precariousness of incomprehensibility.

A woman has her handkerchiefs, her bed, her stockings. She thinks of going back to the house or to the woods for a moment. Nothing changes if I perceive her existence as transparency, as a gamble, or in fact as chance. Her truth isn't above her. But like the "teacup," I reach her only in the few moments of chance. She is a voice in which the world answers me. Although—unless I'm infinitely attentive, and unless there's a transparence associated with the excesses that drain off suffering—I wouldn't understand a thing.

In carnal love we ought to love excesses of suffering. Without them no risk would exist. In divine love the limitation of suffering is given in divine perfection.

I love irreligiousness, the disrespect involved in risk taking and gambling.

In risk taking, I sometimes push my luck so far that I lose even anguish as a possibility. Anguish in this case would be withdrawal from risk. Love is my necessity. I'm impelled to drift into happiness, sensing chance there. First rapturously to win—then laceratingly to let go of the winnings—in a game that exhausts me.

To encourage bitterness in those last words—words of renewed anguish—would be to avoid taking risks.

I can't take risks without this anguish of feeling suspended. But to take risks means to overcome anguish.

I'm afraid this apology will only encourage foolishness and banal rhetoric. Love is simple, uncomplicated.

My wish is that in any love of the unknown (and no matter what its personal sources in me may be, it arises from mystical traditions) we can, by ousting transcendence, attain such great simplicity as to relate that love to an earthly love, echoing it to infinity.

VI

WHAT FINALLY remains unknown is at one and the same time what I recognize: myself, suspended at the moment of certitude. Myself, in the appearance of a person I am in love with, the sound of a spoon striking a bowl, of the void.

Right away, the beloved gets strangely confused with me. Moreover—once seen this beloved becomes incomprehensible. All the pursuing, finding, and embracing of the person with whom I'm in love, what good does any of it do? I suspected it all along . . . But without first drowning my anguish in sensuality, how could I have endured these torments of desire?

Pain flows from the beloved's obstructions of that love. The beloved turns aside—is different from me.

But without this difference, this abyss—*my recognition of this beloved would have been in vain.* Identity still remains in effect. Only when our response to desire remains incomprehensible is that response true. A response that is understood destroys desire. These limits define desire (define us). We are to the degree that we risk ourselves. If the risk ceases, if I withdraw some aspect to keep it from changing, the resulting regularity will be misleading: I'll pass from the tragic to the ridiculous.

Essentially all beings are only one.
They repel each other at the same time that they are one. And in this movement (their essence), fundamental identity is annulled.

An awareness of déjà vu signifies the sudden and short-lived suspension of a basic movement of repulsion.

Repulsion in us, once a thing comes to be, is the stable aspect.

The stable aspect of isolation is disequilibrium and is thus like every other state.

Our desire defines our luck: it is transparency or the place where opacity is resolved. (Physical beauty is transparent if passive, while an active ugliness in males creates transparency by reversing it.)

Transparency isn't the abolition of individual isolation but transcends it. It is not a *state* of theoretical or fundamental unity, but a chance that occurs in risk.

Chance commingles with a feeling of déjà vu.

Not pure *unified being* but one that is separated is its object, a separated being that owes to chance alone (to itself occurring as a separate being) the power it has to deny separation. But this negation assumes the encounter with a beloved. It's effective only when one person is in the presence of another, supposing in that other the same chance—and in a sense heightening the separation, suspending it solely for the person you choose.

The individual chosen in that election surpasses the universe—the glory of which would be only the splendor of unified being and would be without randomness. But chance belonging to the beloved (what it is) assumes love. To say of the person I fall in love with that this individual actually differs from whatever is given to her or him by love would reveal a common defect in judgments made about people. The beloved person exists *in* this love. To exist for a single person, for a crowd, for so many "boyfriends" or "girlfriends": each of these existences is a different reality, though each is equally real. Love, crowds, social relations, these are all differing realities upon which our existence depends.

In love, chance is first *sought out* by the lover in the beloved. Though chance is also given as the two meet. In a sense the love uniting them celebrates a return to being. It possesses at the same time, though to a supreme degree, the opposite characteristic of being suspended, in autonomy, in the surpassing of risk.

VII

I LOATHE monks.

For me, turning away from the world, from chance, from the truth of bodies is shameful.

No greater sin exists.

Happiness, remembering the night of drinking and dancing, dancing by myself like a peasant, a faun, with couples all around me.

Alone? Actually: There we were dancing face to face in a potlatch of absurdity, the philosopher—Sartre—and me.

I remember whirling about, dancing.

Jumping, stomping down the wooden floor.

Acting rebellious and crazy—like a fool.

For me, there's a connection between this dance, with Sartre opposite me, and a painting I recall (Picasso's *Demoiselles d'Avignon*). The third character was a store-window dummy made out of a horse's skull and a flowing, striped yellow and mauve dressing gown. A grimly medieval canopied bed presiding over the fun.

Five months of nightmare ended in a carnival.

What a surprise—fraternizing like that with Sartre and Camus (I'm talking like a schoolboy).

On the other hand the relationship I see with Zen monks doesn't really encourage me either (they do not dance, drink, or . . . you know what).

In a society of lighthearted free thinking, trusting Zen might be premature. The most attractive Zen monks were chaste.

April–June 1944

To what extent is morality's self-destruction itself a sign of ongoing strength? We Europeans have within us the blood of those who died for their faith; we've taken morality terribly seriously; there is nothing we haven't sacrificed for it. On the other hand, our intellectual refinement is due principally to a vivisection of our conscience. We still don't know where we'll have to go leaving this ancient territory. But this soil, having communicated a strength to us, now aimlessly pushes us toward shoreless climes that remain as yet unexploited and undiscovered; we have no choice, and we're forced to be conquerors because we no longer have a country we want to remain in. A secret confidence impels us, confidence stronger than our negations. Our very strength doesn't allow us to stay on this ancient soil; we'll take a chance, start risking ourselves; the world's still full of treasures, and it's better to perish than become weak and vicious. Our very vigor drives us to high seas where all suns until now have set; we know that there's a new world . . .

—1885–86

I

I AM acting in such a way that the moment I yearn for, the one I await in tears—so to speak—escapes me now. For this reason I go beyond my means. No traces remain in my memory—or few enough. I do not write this in disappointment or anger, but like a drawn arrow, sure of reaching the target.

What I am saying here can be understood—provided that you are possessed of purity so true it can't be lived.

Infinite misunderstanding. What I love—what makes me cry out like a lark with joy to the sun—this forces me to speak it out in melancholy words.

II

Going back—I copy out older sections of this diary dating from over a year ago. In January 1943 (arriving at Vézelay) for the first time I described the chance I speak of—

WHAT BOTHERS me is thinking and thinking—without letup— about all possibility. The future considered weighty and ponderous. But:

Writhing in anguish, however clever I am at bringing up doubts, doubts on anything that would apply (especially the necessity for having resources, this being connected to the pathos of the *Phenom- enology of Mind*—of the class struggle: I would eat if . . .; at the start of 1943, the pathos of events comes to my aid—especially events still to come), nothing would allow me to be untrue to my heart (deep in this heart of mine, a lightness, surge).

No one's more lacerated than I am, seeing, understanding. Sen- sing infinity as I do, making no exceptions, relating this anguish of mine to the rights of the poor, to their anger, to their rage. How could I not ascribe all powers to poverty? Even though poverty could not crush the dancing in my heart, the laughter rising from the depths of despair.

Hegelian Dialectic. Today, between two points, it is impossible for me not to be a hyphen, a leap, for an instant resting on nothing.

The leap won out on all counts. Stendhal gaily subverted his resources (the society that was the basis of these resources). Then comes a time to settle the score.

In the process the human figures you see in the air between the two points are crossed out—they aren't there now.

Two descriptions contradict each other. I described myself in the first paragraph as free from the anguish of having to settle the score.

To spell this out further—

Leaping is life. Settling the score is death.

And if history stops, I die.

Or . . .

Beyond settling the score, is there some new kind of leap? If history is over, is there a leap outside of time as I keep on shouting "Time is out of joint."

In a state of extreme anguish—and then decisively—I wrote the following poems:

> *Out of my mind*
> *shouting what is*
> *this hopelessness*
>
> *in my heart*
> *the dead mouse*
> *hidden*
>
> *the mouse dead*
> *hunted down*
>
> *and in my hand the world is dead*
> *the old candle blown out*
> *as I go upstairs to bed*
>
> *the illness the death of this world*
> *I am this illness*
> *I am the death of this world.*
>
> *The silence in my heart*
> *with winds blowing violently*
> *my head throbbing with death*
> *and a star a black grave*
> *inside my not-yet-toppled-over skeleton*
>
> *black*
> *quiet I invade the sky*

my black mouth
is an arm
the blackness of
writing on a wall
in black flames
empty winds from a grave
whistling about my head.

Demented silence as I
put one foot after the other
the silence of a gulp
taking in heaven and earth

delirious heaven
I'm going crazy

I push the world
off course
and I die
I forget about it I bury it
in the grave of my bones.

nobody is home
in these Jolly Roger eyes
of mine.

Hope
oh my rocking horse
in the dark a giant
that's me the giant
on a rocking horse.

Starry sky
my sister
accursed species humankind
star you're death
oh cold cold light

loneliness like lightning
the human species gone at last

I drain off their memories
a forsaken sun
wipes out my name

I can see this star
its freezing silence
howls wolfishly
on my back I'm falling down
onto the earth
killing me
I know you, oh earth.

Oh the dice thrown
from the bottom of the grave
by the fingers of the cunning night

dice like birds of the sun
leaps of drunken larks
I go forth an arrow
shooting out
of the night

oh transparency of bones
my heart drunk with sunlight
is the shaft of night.

III

I'M ASHAMED of myself. There's something soft about me, easily swayed . . . I'm not young any more.

A few years ago I was tough, filled with bravado, with a take-charge attitude. It seems that's over with and was shallow, perhaps. Back then there wasn't that much risk in action and affirmation!

My ability to bounce back seems gone for good:

war crushes my hopes (nothing functions outside the political systems);

illness is wasting me away;

unrelenting anguish ends up playing havoc with my nerves (I can't regard this development as a weakness);

at a moral level I feel reduced to silence (the summit can't be asserted—no one can speak in its name).

What counters this is a consciousness that's sure of itself. If any chance of action exists, I'll risk it—not as an ancillary risk, but as a risk of my life. Even if I'm older, sick, and feverish, it's not in my nature to simply sit by and do nothing. I can't keep endlessly accepting this infinitely monstrous sterility which fatigue brings to my life.

(Under my present living conditions, the slightest lapse of awareness brings on giddiness. At 5 A.M. I'm cold, my heart sinks, what is there to do but sleep?)

As for the subject of life and death: sometimes I bitterly eye the worst, I stake my bet, helplessly slip into horror. I know all is lost. And I know that dawn, a potential illuminator, will cast its light on a dead man.

Inside me everything laughs blindly at life. Buoyant like a child: walking through life, carrying it.

I hear the rain falling.

My depressed state, the threats of death, some kind of destructive fear that also shows the way to the summit—all these whirl in me, haunting and choking me . . . But I am—we are—going to go on.

IV

I SURPRISE myself by falling into anguish . . . But still!

I never stop taking risks—this is the condition for the intoxication of heart.

Which indeed is a confrontation with the sickening depths in things. To risk is to touch life's limit, go as far as you can, live on the edge of gaping nothingness!

Free and choosing freedom, the free spirit chooses between asceticism and risk. Asceticism is the risk implied in adverse chance—it's the negation of that risk, it's the risk reversed. To be sure, asceticism is renunciation and withdrawal from risk. Although withdrawal is itself risk.

In the same way, risk is kind of a renunciation. The sum risked by real gamblers is lost as a type of "resource," not to be gambled again. If you lose this sum, there's nothing more to say. But in winning, if gain is added, further stakes to be gambled are created, and that remains the sole possibility. "Money burns a hole in my pocket" when I gamble. Excited by the betting, I dedicate myself to gambling. (To play from formula or mathematical speculations is the opposite of gambling as a calculus of chance probabilities.)

In the same way—as desire sets me on fire, intoxicating me, as my pursuit of the object of my desire becomes a risk—deep inside me I utterly lose hope. Like the winnings of a gambler, sexual possession prolongs desire—or extinguishes it. "From now on I'll get no rest!"

The holiness of the romanticism of gambling, unlike that of asceticism, makes monks and abstainers tepid.

"Failure should be honored *because* it is failure. . . ." Thus does Nietzsche speak on the subject of remorse in *Ecce Homo*.

What is odd in Nietzsche's doctrines is that they can not be followed. Ahead of you are unfocused, at times dazzling radiances. Though the way to them remains untraceable.

Nietzsche the prophet of new paths? But *superman* and *eternal return* are empty as motives of excitement or action, are inadequate compared to Christian and Buddhist motives. The *will to power* is in fact a paltry subject for consideration. Having it is one thing—but this doesn't mean you should give it your attention.

What Nietzsche perceived was the falseness of preachers telling us to do this or that, using language to depict evil, exhorting us to struggle. "My experience," he says (*Ecce Homo*), "knows nothing about 'willing,' 'working ambitiously,' keeping in mind some 'goal' or realizing some desire." What could be more contrary to the propaganda of Christians and Buddhists?

Compared to Zarathustra, Jesus and Buddha look slavish. They had "something they had to do" in the world, and their tasks might even be called overpowering. They were only "wise," "knowing," or "Saviors." Zarathustra (Nietzsche) is more: he is a seducer, laughing at the tasks he undertook.

Imagine a friend of Zarathustra's showing up at the monastery and, being refused, sitting at the entry gate, awaiting acceptance (all in good time) from authorities. Now, the issue is not just one of being humble, lowering one's head, not laughing. Buddhists and Christians are united in taking with great seriousness whatever they commence—and no matter how strong their desires they vow to stop knowing women! Jesus and Buddha had "something they had to do" in the world: they assigned their disciples an arid and obligatory task.

In the end, the only knowledge Zarathustra's students gain is to repudiate their master. For it is said to them they should hate him and "raise their hand against his crown." For the follower, the danger isn't the prophet's admonition to "live dangerously" but not having "something to do" in this world.

You have to decide. Either you do not believe in what you can do (what you actually can do, but without faith). Or you are not the student of Zarathustra—who allots no tasks.

In a cafe where I go to have dinner—overhearing the following domestic squabble. Outside, the boss, a silly young husband, complaining about his wife: "Why does she have to pout like that?" Inside, the wife, serving customers, her face knit in a tense smile.

Everywhere the conflict of things explodes. But isn't this something we desire? Even the conflict between K and me: opening inside me like a wound, it's a never-ending flight robbing me of life, leaving me like someone falling on some unseen step. And despite my fears, this is what I want. When K suddenly sweeps in, staring with nonchalant stares—at times I'm aware of burning complicity within me. Likewise today. Though perhaps on the verge of nervous breakdown, I still can't deny a subdued desire for, and expectation of, the ordeals that (irrespective of their results) I know are coming.

If I possessed within me musical resources to communicate my feelings, what would eventuate would be a (quite probably feeble) explosion—an explosion that, at one and the same time, would be both a languorous demented wave of sound and the expression of wild joy—a joy so untamed, however, that listening to it there would be no way of knowing if it came from my laughing or dying.

V

SUDDENLY THE time has come. Difficulties, bad luck, great if disappointing enthusiasms—to which should be added threatening trials. I vacillate. And if it develops that I will have to remain alone— how, in that case, to go on with my life . . . I don't know.

Or rather I do know. I will stick it out. I will not take my failings that seriously. I will go on as before. Though at present I'm a bundle of nerves. In a bad way from drinking. Unhappy at being alone and waiting. Trials becoming unbearable, not because they are the effect of some misfortune but because they stem only from disappearing chance.

(Chance—so fragile and always posing risks—fascinates, exhausts me.)

I'll get a grip on it, I'll go on with my life (I have already begun)— and the condition required for this is action! I'm being very careful about my words now—as if the effort involved might be worth it.

Provided that I am able to act!

As well as have "something to do"!

How else to get a grip on and endure the emptiness, the feelings of pointlessness, the unappeasable desires? And what exactly would there be to do, if not write this . . . write this book? Wherein I've told of disappointment (despair) arising from not having "something to do" in this world.

But at the very bottom of failure (a buoyant failure, it's true), there's something I vaguely discern.

I have a goal in this world that impels me to act.

It can't be defined.

I imagine an arduous path marked by tribulation, and on it

gleaming chance never forsakes me. I picture the inevitable, all the events still to come.

From laceration or nausea, my knees weak even at the last moment, I'll take a chance on . . .

The chance that's my lot, that tirelessly renews itself, the chance that day by day went on before me

like a herald before a knight

The chance that nothing can limit, that I evoke when I write of

myself like an arrow
shooting out in the night

the chance connecting me to someone I love, for better or for worse. This chance needs to be gambled away, risked in its entirety.

And if by chance you see a chance beside me, take it!
It's your chance, not mine.
No more than I, can you grasp this chance.
You'll know nothing about it, though you take a chance on it.
In fact who sees it without gambling?

You, whoever you are, reading me—take your own chance.
As I do, with all deliberation. Just as, at the moment of writing, I gamble with you.
This chance isn't yours or mine. It belongs to all humanity, to human light.
And has it ever before possessed such brilliance as the night now confers on it?

No one except K and M (if even K and M, for that matter) can know the significance of these verses (or the previous lines):

the dice of sun-birds

(On another level they're also empty of meaning.)

I gamble at the edge of a pit so great only depths of dreams, only nightmares of dying, can define it.

In fact risk is first of all a refusal to take anything seriously. And dying . . .

Individual assertion, compared to risk or chance, seems empty and inopportune.

It's a shame to limit something essentially unlimited—chance and risk.

It's possible for me to think that K or X can't *gamble* without me (the converse is true, I could not *gamble* without K or X). That doesn't mean anything definite (unless "taking your chances" is "discovering who you are"; "discovering the person that you are" is "finding the chances that you were"; "the chances that you were" is reached only "in gambling").

So that now . . .?

If I define the type of person who is worthy of love, I only halfheartedly desire to be understood.

Definition betrays desire. Its aim is the inaccessible summit. But the summit eludes any attempt to think about it. It's *what is*. Never *what should be*.

Once assigned to a particular place, the summit is reduced to individual convenience. It bears on the person's interest. Which, in religion, is salvation. Of myself or others.

Two of Nietzsche's definitions:

1) "AN ELEVATED STATE OF SOUL—It seems to me that people generally do not believe in elevated states of soul, unless momentarily or at best over short periods of time—making exception for those few individuals who from experience know these elevated feelings in duration. But to be a person with a single elevated feeling, the incarnation of some unique, great state of soul—that, till now, has been just a dream and delightful possibility, because history still hasn't given us clear examples of this. Nonetheless, the possibility

exists that history still will bring such beings into existence. Who will occur as the favorable series of conditions is created and determined, a series which at present even the most favorable luck can't bring about. And with such future souls, as it may be, the exceptional state, that from time to time takes hold of us as we tremble, will be precisely the normal condition; a continual shunting back and forth between high and low, a feeling of heights and depths, of ceaselessly mounting steps and soaring above clouds." (*Gay Science*)

2) "Souls with the greatest range, that go deepest,

the largest souls, those that can run, amble, wander into the furthest reaches of themselves,

the most necessary souls, as they are hurled pleasureably toward chance,

souls that are and want to enter becoming, souls having will and desire, and wanting to hurtle into those states,

souls escaping themselves and making their way back to themselves around the greatest circuits,

the wisest souls, to whose hearts derangement speaks with utmost gentleness,

souls which are the most in love with themselves and within which all things have their rise and fall, their flux and reflux." (Zarathustra)

The factual existence of these souls can't be denied without sufficient reason.

They are different from mystics because of their risking and gambling, because they are not the result of calculation that plots outcomes.

What does it mean that earlier I provoked K like that?

But it's not something I can help!

For me it's actual truth.

"You're like a part of me, a piece of living flesh. If you fail your own exaltedness, I get uneasy. In another sense it's a relief. But if we fail each other, this has to take place along a spectrum (we can, we must diverge from each other, although only if—going the limit without any calculation—we risk and gamble ourselves). I know there's no such thing as *obligation* in this world, yet inside me, I cannot repress the awareness of my uneasiness, derived from fear of risk, of gambling . . ."

The bottom line is: Anyone and everyone is part of me.

Fortunately, we usually don't notice this.

But lovemaking brings out this truth.

Within me, only a faltering is left, only a burning ardor, only living and dying—because of my hope.

For those I'm attached to, I'm a provocation. I can't stand seeing them forget the *chance* they would be if they took risks.

Senseless hopes excite me.

Before me I see a sort of flame, a flame that is me, that kindles me.

"I'd like to bring harm on those I illuminate."

Incapable of doing anything—I survive—in laceration. And with my eyes, I follow a shimmering light that turns me into its plaything.

"If we're at all superstitious, it's hard not to have the feeling of being only an incarnation, a megaphone or medium, for higher powers. The idea of revelation—if by that you understand a sudden appearance of something making you see and hear it with sharpness and inexpressible precision, overwhelming everything within you, overcoming you in your innermost being—this idea of revelation corresponds to a specific fact. There is such a thing as hearing without searching; as taking without inquiring as to who might be giving; and thought flashes forth like lightning, imposed as a necessity, under a definitive form: I have never had to choose. With such raptures, our too weary souls ease themselves, sometimes in a torrent of tears; mechanically we begin, and we speed up or slow down without realizing it; in such ecstasies we're ravished from ourselves, and hundreds of delicate feelings crisscross, penetrating us down to our toes; in this abyss of felicity, horror and extreme suffering never appear as contraries of, but as results of, the glimmerings of such happiness, and as a hue that would necessarily suffuse the bottom of this ocean of light . . ." (*Ecce Homo*)

I can't imagine a "higher power." In its simplicity I see chance as unendurable, benevolent, and ardent . . .

And without it, a person would be what he or she is.

What must be intuited in shadows before us—the enchanting appeal of some milky beyond, the certainty of a lake of delights.

VI

QUESTIONING THAT takes place in failure requires an immediate response. I have to live rather than continue to know. Questioning that desires knowledge (defined as torment) supposes putting aside real concerns: it occurs as life is suspended.

I can now easily see what (more or less) turns each of us away from possibility. Or, if you will, what turns us from ourselves.

Possibility in fact is simply chance—chance that can't be grasped without danger, since that would be the equivalent of accepting life as lifelessness and taking as something dangerous the truth of life that is chance. Chance involves rivalry and brazenness. Hence, our hatred of sublimity, our deep-rooted assertion of the quotidian, our fears of the ridiculous (transitory feelings, stymieing us, that we are afraid to let ourselves have). A false, vague, devious attitude, balking at impropriety, even shunning the signs of life that generally characterize manliness (maturity and particularly conversations), can be regarded as the panicked fear of *chance* and risk, the fear of human possibility—of all we claim to love in humanity and understand as the occurrence of chance and reject when we assume false, impervious attitudes—all that we understand as chance risking itself, disequilibrium, intoxication, dementia.

That's the situation. Each of us involved in killing the humanness inside us. To live life and demand it, and to make life echo resoundingly, thwarts our own interests. To say to those around you, "Take a good look at yourselves—bleary-eyed, bent over, ever holding back, lackluster, accepting infinities of boredom, lacking pride—that is what you do with possibility; as you read you express admiration, but within and around you, you kill whatever you claim you like (what you like only when it is dead and gone and not actively a temptation to you), you love possibility in books but I read in your eyes a hatred for chance . . ."—to speak that way would be ridiculous and would go against the current for no purpose, ranting and raving. Love that asks for chance—that desires to be loved—also asks us to love the inability to love chance, which is in what chance rejects.

I don't in the least hate God—I know nothing at all about him. If God was what they say, he would be *chance*. To me, it's as much of a cheap trick to transform chance into God as the opposite would be for a churchgoer. God can't be *chance*—since he's everything. But chance, as it comes to be is endlessly risk, has no knowledge of itself insofar as it comes to be, and so rejects itself in this coming to be (it's warfare itself), wants as much to love and be loved as churchgoers believe is the case with God. Or, better: compared to the urgencies of chance, God's necessities are child's play! For chance raises us up to heights only to hurl us down; finally, we can hope for only one grace—that chance will tragically destroy us and not let us die in our lethargy.

When pious falsifiers set up divine love against creature love, they pit chance against God and oppose what occurs (what is being risked) to the crushing totality of a world that already has occurred.

CREATURE LOVE IS ALWAYS THE SIGN OF, AND PATH TOWARD, AN INFINITELY TRUER, INFINITELY MORE LACERATING, INFINITELY PURER LOVE THAN THE DIVINE LOVE. (To the extent of being a developed figure, God is envisaged as simply the foundation of merit, the substitution of guarantees for chance.)

For those who grasp what chance is, the idea of God seems insipid and suspicious, like being crippled.

To endow God, who is everything, with the attributes of chance(!): this slippery aberration intellectually and psychologically supposes a crushing of our creaturehood (a creature is human chance).

VII

I WRITE sitting on a wharf, legs propped up on ship's ballast. I'm waiting. I hate waiting. Not much hope of getting there on time. This tension . . . so ridiculously . . . in conflict with desires to live! I'm saying that about these downcast thoughts of happiness in the middle of a despondent crowd that is waiting—in the shadowy half-light—for day's end.

Got there on time. After three miles through the forest at night. Woke up K, chucking fistfuls of little pebbles against her window. Exhausted.

Paris dull and sluggish after the bombings. Occasional relief, though. Turning to go, S repeated something funny that the building manager told him, "It's a sorry sight, you know, seeing still-living corpses pulled out after the air raids—a capital defense!"

From an account of torture in the newspaper (*Petit Parisien*, 4/27): ". . . eyes gouged out, ears, fingernails ripped off, head bashed in from numerous blows with a log, tongue sliced in two with tongs . . ." As a child, the notion of torture made life miserable for me. Even now I can't say how I'll be able to stand it . . . The earth revolving in its skies . . . Today, everywhere, the earth a carpet of flowers—lilacs, wisteria, iris. But the war drones on: hundreds of planes filling the night, sounding like flies . . .

Sensuality is nothing without an equivocal shift—in which suddenly there is this glimpse of a demented "goo" that, although normally escaping us, suddenly seems attainable. The "goo" still gets away. But in the brief glimpse our hearts beat with deranged hopes. It's such hopes as these that, jumbled all together and pushing forward, finally allow the surging forth of . . . Often, a deranged beyond lacerates us while we're apparently bent on lasciviousness.

This is because a "beyond" begins with a feeling of nakedness. Asexual nakedness is simply stupor taken to the limit. But as it awakens us to an awareness of physical touch (touch of bodies, hands, moist lips), it's gentle, animal, and *sacred* . . .

since, once naked, we each open to more than what we are, and for the first time we obliterate ourselves in the absence of animal limits. We obliterate ourselves, spreading our legs, our legs opening as widely as possible, to what no longer is us but is something impersonal—a swampy existence of the flesh.

The communication of two individuals occurs when they lose themselves in sweet, shared slime . . .

Immense stretches of forest, wild-looking heights.

I lack imagination. Carnage, conflagration, horror, that's what's in store, apparently, in the weeks to come. When I'm walking through woods, over the hills, I can't imagine it all going up in flames. Although it'd catch like straw.

Yesterday from quite far off—the smoke from some sort of fire—in the direction of A.

Meanwhile I'm numbering these most recent days as among the best in my life. So many flowers everywhere. The light unbelievably lovely. And far up in the sunlight—a profusion of oak leaves!

The idea of the sovereignty of desire and anguish (or fear) isn't so easy for us to understand. In fact desire lies hidden. And naturally, anguish is silent (it affirms nothing). If a person thinks of ordinary sovereignty, anguish and desire seem dangerous. If a person thinks of anguish and desire, what connection would there be to sovereignty?

Can sovereignty mean something else? Over and above that? I mean—given the fact that it exercises no dominion over anything, is misunderstood in our confronting of existence, and is even concealed, having only something comical and shameful to it?

But still, I'll describe this kind of autonomy—the autonomy of moments of distress or delight (ecstasy or physical pleasure)—as the type of autonomy least open to doubt. Sexual pleasure (concealing itself and provoking laughter) comes closest to the essence of majesty. Likewise despair.

But neither the desperado nor the sensualist can know what majesty they have. Once known, it's lost. Human autonomy necessarily escapes our being able to perceive it (it would be servile if it openly declared itself). True sovereignty so conscientiously effects a mortal destruction of itself that it can't, even for a moment, pose this mortal self-destruction as a real question.

"No men around here. I'm gonna go and find one" (an American woman). Saying that requires more virtue than refusing temptation.

When drinking, it's natural to flow into the next person. Stinginess becomes a vice, the demonstration of poverty (dessication). If it weren't for the power that men have, their power to cast a cloud on things, poison things, go bitter, turn rancorous, boring, and small-minded, what excuse would there be for female caution? Work, anxieties, and immense love . . . the best and worst.

Beautiful sunny day—the summer almost here. Enough sun, heat, and flowers, bodies open up . . .

Nietzsche's weakness. He criticizes from the standpoint of a *moving* value, whose origin and end he—obviously—doesn't grasp.

To grasp an isolated possibility that has a private end, one that's an end to itself, isn't this essentially to risk, or to gamble?

So maybe the interesting aspect of this has to do with the aspect of risk rather than the end chosen.

What if, strictly speaking, this procedure lacked an end? Risk would mark out values just the same.

The *superman* or Borgia side of things is limited and vainly defined in relation to possibilities whose essence is a going beyond self.

(This in no way detracts anything from the pell-mell rush, the roaring wind that upsets all old certainties.)

Tonight—physically played out, feeling strange and upset. Always waiting... Certainly this isn't the right time for any self-examination. But why fight this? Against all inclination and out of fatigue, from restlessness, questioning myself, in my present state of suspension where anything and everything is posed as a question—under such conditions, the only fear concerning that distant possibility is whether I'm capable of going the limit. What does failure mean if, nonetheless, it is so easily overcome? In every way I'll be a failure—attributing to my weakness the fleeting results.

I keep at it. The calm returns at last, and I get back a sense of control, a feeling that the only way to be fate's toy is to be in alignment with risk.

Go the limit? Right now, I'm only randomly making progress. A little while ago, out walking along the lane, a country road lined with chestnut trees, flames of nonmeaning opened up the limits of the sky... But it's to the immediate questions, all the same, that I have to respond. *What to do?* How to relate my ends to some sort of activity that never wavers? How to lead full being into emptiness?

After a pure exhilaration the other day comes this immediate anxiety. It's not unexpected. Again—the waiting crushes me.

Just now with K assessing the situation... For a moment (all too fleeting) we were happy. The possibility of some infinite void haunts me. I'm aware of an implacable situation, the future with no outcome (This time, I don't mean the events near at hand).

Will there be another, more ponderous situation? At another time? It's not clear.

Today everything is naked.

What rested on artifice is destroyed.

The night we're entering isn't simply the dark night of John of the Cross, isn't just the empty universe bereft of a helpful God—it's the night of real hunger, of the cold we feel in our rooms, of something that seems glaringly obvious in police stations.

This overlap of three different desperations is worth contemplating. To be concerned about the beyond of chance seems to me to lack any rights, compared to the needs of the many. And I know there isn't any recourse—and that ghosts of desire only increase the suffering.

How under these conditions to justify the world? Or better—how to justify *me?* How can there be *a desire to exist?*

Uncommon strength is necessary. But if I didn't already have strength at my disposal, I wouldn't have grasped this situation in its nakedness.

What takes me way down. My daily anguish.

Sweetness. Or rather my delight in life.

Constant, inevitable alarms in dealing with my personal life—and as my delight increases, so do the alarms.

The value assumed by delight when, from out of everywhere, some impossibility is looming.

The fact that, given the slightest weakness, everything falls through—at the same time.

The enthusiasm that impels this writing of mine brings up Goya's *El Dos de Mayo.* That's not a joke. Very little in the painting refers to night—and it's flashingly bright. My present happiness is solid. I feel strength as the worst tries me. Laughing at anything and everything.

Otherwise I'd fall, with nothing to catch me, into definitive void.

The void is tempting to me. But *what do I do* in the void?

Becoming something that's put to one side, an outmoded firearm, something superseded by a newer model. Giving in to the self-disgust.

Without my happiness—without flashing brightness—I fall. I'm chance and light, gently staving off inevitability.

And otherwise?

Subject to infinite sufferings without meaning.

For that reason I'd suffer doubly if I lost K. She reaches not simply my passion but my nature (essence).

I awake anguished over yesterday's bewilderment. Forgetfulness is always depressing—mine signifies fatigue. Is it from abnormal living conditions? Is the fatigue related to despair? Even enthusiasm comes close to despair.

The shallowness of my anguish: perseverance is stronger. The fact of having resolutely put it into words makes my perseverance tangible, something that doesn't change from yesterday to this morning. Passion in a sense remains secondary. Or rather, it turns into a decisiveness. Passion degrades life when absorbing it. It bets *everything*, all life, on partial stakes. Pure passion being a little like a female orchestra—something is missing, the void enters. The risk I imagine, on the contrary, is total, it brings everything into question, the life of every individual, the future of the knowable world. Even the void seen in loss in this case would be the response that could be expected to infinite desire, to an occurrence of infinite death: a void so large it discourages you to the point of despair.

Today, the issue confronting us isn't the disappearance of lucid and cynical—or strong—natures. It's simply the uniting of these natures with the totality of being, at the limits of understanding and experiencing possibility.

In each area, consideration must be given to:

1) the average generally available or available for the specific group—thus the average standard of living or the average output;

2) the extremity, the maximum, or the summit.

Humanly speaking, neither of these opposing considerations can be eliminated. The group viewpoint has to be factored in by the individual—and so does the individual viewpoint by the group.

If one of these viewpoints is rejected, this is done tentatively—under certain conditions.

These considerations are clear in what relates to particular areas (physical exercise, intelligence, culture, technical abilities . . .). They aren't as clear when the factor involved is life generally. Or what can be expected from life. Or, if you will, a way of living that is worth our liking it (worth our seeking it out and worth our vaunting it). Without speaking of diverging opinions, a final difficulty emerges from the fact that the daily life that is being considered differs qualitatively—and not just quantitatively—depending on whether we are looking at an average or an extreme. There exist in fact two kinds of extreme: one that from the outside seems extreme to the average, and another that seems extreme to those who themselves have some experience with extremity.

Here again, *humanly*, there's no doing away with either viewpoint.

But if the average has no right to eliminate the viewpoint of pure extremity, it's no less acceptable for extremity to reject the existence and rights of average viewpoints.

I'll go further.

Extremity can't be attained if you imagine a group *required* to recognize extremity as such (Rimbaud thinking of the mob as diminished by the fact of its being unaware of and misconstruing Rimbaud!).

Still:

By the same token there's no extremity that lacks recognition on the part of others (although this isn't the extremity *of* the others: I'm referring to the Hegelian principle of *Anerkennen*). The possibility of being recognized by a significant minority (Nietzsche) is already within the night, to which, finally, all extremity must move.

In the end only chance has the possibility of openness.

VIII

F ROM THE multitude of life's difficulties flows infinite possibility. And when difficulties bring us up short, we attribute this to the feeling of impossibility controlling us!

If we think of existence as unbearable, it's on account of some specific mishap leading us astray.

And we struggle against this mishap.

The impossible gets dismissed when struggle is possible.

If I claim the summit, I can't regard it as attained.

Just the opposite—since (tragically?) I feel I have to say:

Nietzsche's powerlessness can't be appealed.

If possibility is given us in chance (and isn't received from outside but is the possibility that we are, the possibility that forces us to take risks by forcing us to the very end) there clearly isn't anything of which it could be said, "It will be possible like this." It won't be possible but risked. And chance or risk essentially assumes what is impossible.

The tragedy of Nietzsche is the tragedy of night emerging from excesses of light.

His eyes emboldened and wide open, like an eagle in flight: the sun of immorality and dazzling malice left him blinded.

A dazzled man speaks to you.

The most difficult thing.

Getting as far down as possible.

Down to where everything thrown to the ground is shattered. Your nose in a puddle of vomit.

Rising again—without shame—to heights of friendship.

Wherever the strength and tension of willpower are useless, there chance laughs (The precise awareness of possibility, the harmony ordained by hazard—or . . . ?). Chance laughs, raising its innocent finger . . .

It actually seems strange to me.
Personally I'm coming to the point of the greatest darkness.
Where everything appears destroyed.
Against all eventuality: raised by a feeling of chance!
That would be impotent hypocrisy if anguish hadn't worn me down.

The most ponderous aspect of it.
Admitting Nietzsche's defeat and blind error, his impotence.
A bird burned up in the light. The stench of scorched feathers.
Human intelligence is weak, it sallies forth in battle.
Which isn't a situation we can avoid.
So. We expect love to be a solution—for infinite suffering. And what choice do we have? Within us the anguish is infinite, and we fall in love. Is there some other alternative—other than comically making love on a Procrustean bed? Infinite anguish!

The only strict and honest path.
Making no finite demands. Conceding no limitation—regardless of the way chosen. Not even when striking out toward infinity. Demanding of an individual that this person be whatever he or she is, or will be. Knowing nothing except fascination. Never stopping at the apparent limit.

IX

YESTERDAY EVENING drank two bottles of wine together with K. The night a wonderland in moonlight and storm. Forest—night— pools of moonlight along a road through the trees—on the embankment little phosphorescent patches. Striking a match—portions of worm-eaten branches inhabited by glowworms. Never knew a happiness so pure, so wild and dark. Awareness of going quite far—and coming to impossibility. The fascinating impossible. As if in the night we'd gotten lost.

Coming back alone, climbing on the rocks.

The idea that there's no necessity in the world of objects, that ecstasy might be adequate to the world (and not God or objects to a mathematical necessity) appeared to me for the first time. Lifting me off the ground.

Atop the rocks in fierce wind, taking off the clothes I had on (because of the heat—just a shirt and pants). The wind tearing at the clouds and by moonlight pushing and pulling them into first one shape, then another. The immense forest under moonlight. Turning, looking out to . . . in hopes of . . . (lost interest in being naked, put on my clothes once more). Existences (a lover or myself) slowly losing themselves into death like clouds unraveling in the wind— never again . . . I loved K's face. Like clouds unraveling in the wind: soundlessly I entered ecstasy, reduced to a dead point, resulting in all the more clarity.

A night of fascination (not many others like it).

The horrible night at Trento (the old men, handsome, dancing like gods—the storm letting loose, while I watched, from a room in which hell . . . the window opened on the Duomo and the palaces along the square).

At night a little public square at V, atop the hill, to me not unlike the square at Trento.

Nights in Vézeley as entrancing as that other night—and one of them was filled with agony.

A certain decision, which was confirmed by a poem about the dice (written at Vézeley), connects with Trento.

The particular night in the forest was equally decisive.

Chance—an incredible series of chances—has been my companion for ten years now. Lacerating and wrecking my life, and leading it to the edge of the abyss. Certain types of chance force you to live at the edge: with a little more anguish, chance would become mischance.

X

LEARNED ABOUT the landing. The news didn't penetrate—it slowly sank in.

Went back to my room.

A hymn to life.

Would I have felt like laughing yesterday?

A toothache (over with now, it seems).

This morning. Still some fatigue. My mind a blank. The last of the fever. Feelings of impotence. Afraid of the possibility of no more news.

I'm calm, emptied. Hope in important events keeps me even-keeled and steady.

All the same, taken aback in this solitude. Resigned. Relative indifference to my personal life.

Ten days ago, on the contrary, returning from Paris, I was surprised . . . I've got to the egotistic stage of wanting stability right now! No, just the opposite. I'm ruling out even the thought of rest today—though, even so, that's what's probable.

Sounds from distant bombs (these becoming commonplace). No option for me but to spend twelve uninterrupted days, alone and without friends, staying in my room, depressed and vulnerable to gnawing anguish.

What about connecting with someone? Finding my life again? My shame about anguish related to the idea of chance. To be honest: under present conditions connecting up would be the only authentic chance, the full "state of grace" that is chance.

For a man, loving a woman (or some other kind of passion) is the sole means of not being God. The priest adorned in arbitrary ornamentation isn't God either—something in him pukes out logic, vomits out God's *necessity*. An officer, a bellboy, etc., submits to the arbitrary.

I suffer—because happiness might be taken away tomorrow. Whatever life remained in me would then seem empty (empty, truly empty). Should I attempt to fill this void? With another woman? A sickening thought. With a human task? I would be God! Or . . . I'd attempt to be him. As soon as you lose what you love, you're told— work! Submit to this or that reality, live for it (or live for the interest you have in such reality)! But if reality seems empty—what then?

Never before (I'm really reaching the limit of the possible, after so many excesses), have I ever felt myself so intensely under a necessity that compels me to love the essentially perishable and to live under the possibility of losing it.

I am aware of deep moral urgencies.

Today I suffer acutely—knowing that the only way to be God is to be untrue to myself.

Eleven more days of solitude . . . (given that nothing untoward develops). Yesterday afternoon, started on an article I am taking a break from—to emphasize its intent. The light of my life is missing, and I'm desperately working, I'm studying the unity of humanness and the world, I'm making interconnected outlines of knowledge, political action, and unlimited contemplation.

Impossible not to yield to this truth, that my life implies a beyond of light, a beyond of the chance I love.

Still—insanity or utter wisdom demonstrates that the beyond of chance, a beyond that supports me if some immediate chance (someone I love) fails, itself has characteristics of chance.

Normally we deny those characteristics. We can only deny them if we seek some ground or stable foundation so as to endure contingency—a contingency that then becomes reduced to the subordinate role. We track down this "beyond" principally when we suffer. Hence Christianity's superficiality (with attitudes of piety built in from the outset). Hence the necessity of a reduction to reason, of an infinite confidence in systems that eliminate chance (probability theories succeed in doing this apparently).

Utter fatigue.

My life no longer a welling up—without which nonmeaning is present.

A basic difficulty: if welling up is necessary for chance, the light (or chance) fails on that which the welling up depended . . .

The irreducible feature is found in this welling up, which didn't wait for light to occur but stimulated it. Random welling up defines the essence of and beginning of chance. Chance is defined in relation to desire, which itself either gives up in desperation, or "wells up."

Deciding to make use of fictions, I dramatize being, I lacerate its solitude, and in this laceration I communicate.

Or once again: mischance is only humanly viable when dramatized. Drama accentuates a mischance factor in chance, which persists in chance, or proceeds from it. The essence of the dramatic hero is a welling up, a rising to chance (dramatic situations require an elevation, from which to fall) . . .

Once again I'm breaking off the article I began. Confusion as a method. In Café du Taureau I'm drinking too many aperitifs. My neighbor, an old man, wheezing softly like a fly. A family drinks beer around a girl dressed for her first communion. German soldiers in the street pass by quickly. A hooker sits between two workers. ("You both could fool around with me . . .") The (inconspicuous) old man goes on wheezing. Sun, clouds. Women all dressed up, looking like a gray day. The sun naked under the clouds.

Exasperation. Depressed and then excited.

Regaining calm. A little firmness is all it takes.

My life (or rather my lack of one) is my method.

Less and less do I question to know. That's something that pretty much leaves me indifferent. And I live. And I question in order to live. I live out my quest, enduring relatively harsh ordeals (harsh because of the jangled state of my nerves). I see no escape at this point. I'm alone with myself, lacking the previous means of escape (pleasure, excitement). I have to get a grip. If I don't, is there any alternative?

Getting a grip? Easy!
Though . . . I myself in control of myself could scare me.
Shifting to decisiveness, I quickly return to a friendship with myself, gentleness. Hence, the necessity for endless chance.
At this point I can only look for chance and attempt to catch it as I laugh.
Taking risks, going looking for chance—this requires patience, love, and total letting go.

A truly isolated period (ten days left, I'm shut up in my room) starts out this morning for me. (I went out yesterday, the day before.)

Yesterday. Kids following behind, running. One behind a streetcar, the other trailing a bus. What's in their small heads? The same thing as is in my own. A basic difference—a decisiveness on my part (I can't depend on others). Here I am, a *self*: awakening, emerging, from a long period of human infancy, in which people relied on each other for everything. But essentially, this dawn of knowledge and this full possession of self is only night, only powerlessness (impotence).
A short phrase will excessively suggest chance—"Could freedom somehow not be powerless?"
Any activity whose object is simply what can be wholly measured is powerful but slavish. Freedom derives from hazard. If we adapt the sum of energy produced to the amount necessary to be produced, human potency leaves nothing to desire, in that it suffices and represents the satisfaction of needs. However, that sort of adaptation would be characterized by constraints, since the distribution of energy to different sectors of production would be stabilized once and for all. But if the amount produced exceeds the necessary, the object of impotent activity is a production that can't be measured.

This morning resigned myself to waiting.

Without fussing, and gently, I came to a decision . . .

Obviously this wasn't reasonable. Still, I left, buoyed up by feelings of chance.

After being encouraged, chance responded to me. Much beyond my hopes.

The horizon clears up (a portion dark).

The wait reduced—from ten to six days.

The game changes. Possibly . . . I knew how to play it today.

Anguish and anxiety preoccupy me and gnaw at me.

Anguish is present and hovering over possible depths . . . I hoist myself up to my summit and see the grounding of things opening up.

Like an unwelcome knock at the door, anguish is present.

Which is the sign of risk and chance.

In its demented voice—chance urging me.

I "well up" out of myself, flames "welling up," right in front of me!

There's no getting around it. My life (under current conditions?), a nightmare, a moral agony.

Which isn't of any account, obviously!

Endlessly, we "annihilate" ourselves—thought and life falling into the void where they dissipate.

To call this void God—this void at which I have aimed, at which my thought aims!

In the prisonhouse of the body what can we do, other than provoke glimpses of something beginning beyond the walls?

My life, strange and exhausting, tonight weighed down with grief.

Spent an hour waiting, suspecting the worst.

Then finally—chance. Though my situation remains implacable.

At midnight opening my window onto the black street, black sky: street, sky, and shadows are crystal clear.

Beyond darkness I easily attain purity, laughter, freedom.

My life recommences.
The lighthearted, familiar shock of it as it hits me.
Dazed, drifting downstream.
K tells me that on the third, after drinking, she went looking for
the key to the reservoir, without luck; discovered herself at about four
in the morning sleeping in the woods, damp.

Unpleasant effects from drinking today.
I'd like (and everything urges me toward this) the course of my life
to be definitively playful, vivacious. Demanding of it a miraculous
gentleness, an atmospheric clarity such as the summit would have.
Transfiguring things around me. In the spirit of play, I imagine to
myself making a pact with K: the lightheartedness of it, the void
itself, transparent (because aimless) emptiness, at some impossible
altitude.
Again to make demands, to act, to realize chance in some specific
way: this corresponds to the "welling up" of desire.
Acting, not with narrow ends but with unlimited ones, glimpsing
chance beyond all my ends as a surpassing of willpower: the practice
of free activity.

Going back over the course of my life.
I see myself slowly reaching a limit.
With anguish waiting for me on all sides, walking a narrow tightrope, raising my eyes heavenward, I perceive a tiny and dazzling
bright light—a star—consuming this anguish of mine. My anguish
waits for me, no matter where I turn.
I possess a power to attract, an infinite power.

This morning I doubted my chance.
As the moment went on and on, in interminable waiting, there
came the dawn of a thought, "All is lost." At the time, it was logical.
I reasoned like this. "My life is a leap, an impulse, whose strength
is chance. At this stage—at the level at which I presently gamble my

life—if I lack chance, I collapse. What am I but a man setting chance possibilities for himself? Didn't I give myself that power—myself? But if misfortune, or mischance, begins for me, the chance giving me that impetus turns out to be merely illusion! I lived believing I had the capacity to fascinate chance, but that wasn't the case." (I had not finished my complaints). "My lightness and distracted victory over anguish were wrongly conceived. I gambled away desire and the will to act (I didn't chose this game) on my chance. Today mischance answers me. I despise ideas dismissed by life itself when these ideas suggest chance as a prominent value . . ."

At the time, I was in a bad way. And a special kind of despair only added (comic) bitterness to my despondency. Is there anything more depressing than waiting? It's an emptiness opening up before you along a path.

As K walked along and spoke with me, my awareness of my misfortune persisted. K was present—I behaved awkwardly. I could hardly believe she was there. And it was hard to think that "my chance lives . . ."

Within me, anguish contests possibility.

My anguish considers vague impossibility to be at odds with my vague desire.

Within me, now, chance and a possibility of chance contest anguish.

Anguish says "impossible," and impossibility depends on whims of chance.

Chance is defined by desire, though not necessarily every response to desire is a chance.

Anguish alone completely defines chance, and chance is what anguish in me regards as impossible.

Anguish can be defined as contesting chance.

Still, I grasp anguish as dependent on whims of chance, which contests, and alone contests, the right of anguish to define us.

After this morning's laceration, my nerves were shattered again (yet again).

Interminable waiting, lighthearted gambling, suspended above the worst eventualities, wracking my nerves, until an interruption makes it even worse . . . There is no helping it, I am compelled to moan in one long groan, "This ode to life and to its glassy transparency!"

Whether despite herself K isn't perhaps manipulating this instability, I can't tell. The confusion she keeps me in seems to stem from her nature.

It's said, "Instead of God there is the impossible—not God." It should be added, "The impossible, which depends on the whims of chance."

Why complain about K?

Chance is endlessly contested, endlessly gambled.

If K had decided to embody chance right down to the last molecule in her, she couldn't have done better. Appearing—although when anguish . . . Then disappearing so suddenly that anguish . . . As if night alone could precede her, as if only night would follow her. But each time without intending it. Appropriately (if she is chance).

"Instead of God, chance." This means nature insofar as it occurs, though not as occurring once and for all but as surpassing itself in infinite occurrences, excluding any possible limits. In this infinite representation (a representation that quite likely is the boldest and most deranged ever tried out by humankind) the idea of God explodes like a bombshell—divine impoverishment and impotence clashing with human chance!

God, a cure applied to anguish (though the anguish can't be healed).

Beyond anguish, dependent on it, defined by it, is chance.

Without anguish—utter anguish—chance wouldn't even be perceived.

"Simply out of appropriateness, if God in fact did exist, he would only be revealed to the world in a human form." (*The Will to Power*)

Being human/human being: to have impossibility opposite you like a wall . . . a wall that chance and only chance could . . .

This morning. Depressed following a night of ungrounded fears, insomnia—sounds of massed planes filling her with dread—K started softly shaking. Frail, despite her appearance of being spirited, playful, and full of zip. Generally, anxiety prevents me from noticing an unfounded distress like this. Empathizing with my woes and hardships—ruts that turn into a way forward for me—she laughed with me good-naturedly. Surprised suddenly to think of her—against the odds—as friend, sister even . . . But had things been otherwise, we would be strangers.

June–July 1944

The wave comes up greedily as if the point were to attain something! With frightening haste creeping far in among the nooks and crannies of a cliff! Something about it seems to desire to raise an alert; apparently something is hidden inside—something valuable, very valued. And now it returns, a bit more slowly, still all white with emotion. Is it disappointed? Did it find what it was looking for? Is it pretending disappointment? But already another wave approaches, more eager, wilder than the first; its soul too seems full of mysteries, full of longing to go seeking treasure. Thus waves live their lives and thus do we—we who possess a will! I won't say a word more.

"What? You mistrust me? You're upset with me, pretty monsters? Afraid that I'll entirely betray your secret? All right then—be annoyed! Raise your greenish, dangerous bodies as high as possible. Build a wall between me and the sun like the one that exists now! Truly, what's left on earth is only green dusk with flashes of green lightning. Do what you want with your impulses, roar with pleasure or spite, you hotheads, or dive and strew emeralds through the depths of the abyss, and on them throw infinite white lace of foam and spume. I approve everything, because everything becomes you, and I'm infinitely pleased with you. How could I betray you? For—listen carefully—I know you and I know your secret, I know what kind of thing you are! You and I . . . we're the same species! You and I . . . we have the same secret!

—*Gay Science*

I

YESTERDAY IN the cafe after eating dinner, young people dancing to accordion music.

An accordionist, his attractive, diminutive head reminding me of that of a mallard, belting out the tune lustily—full of animal vigor, awkward.

I liked him. And I thought, this is what I want for myself, to be a preposterous person and have a bird's eye. A dream—relieving my head as I wrote, like someone relieving his bowels . . . becoming empty like that musician. But that's not the end of the story, since it continues . . . Surrounded by vivacious, pretty young girls, my weightiness (my heart) getting lighter than that *infinite* musician's, I order wine for them. The bar girl announcing, "From an admirer!"

A friend of mine (his soft nature, much to my liking, protecting him from any severity that would exclude a sense of humor) was at Dunkirk in May of 1940. The job assigned to him there for a few days was emptying out the pockets of dead people—to facilitate transferring the contents to the higher-ups. The time came for going on board. The boat finally departed, and my friend scraped alongside the English coast: not far from Dunkirk at Folkstone, the tennis courts alive with athletes in their whites.

And again June 6, departure day, in the center of the town, watching roustabouts put up a merry-go-round.

A little later, in the same place, a convoy of small American planes filled a clear sky. Striped black and white, they whooshed rooftops, machine-gunned roads, and a railroad. Thrilled—and catching my breath.

119

In a rather random way (written as chance and risk dictate) to say this:

That time is the same as being—and being is the same as chance . . . and time.

This signifies that:

If there is time-being, time encloses being in the occurrence of chance individually. The possibilities are apportioned out and oppose each other.

Without individuals, that is to say, without apportioning the possibles, time wouldn't exist.

Time is the same as desire.

The object of desire is for time not to exist.

Time is the desire for time not to exist.

The object of desire is to cancel individuals (others); for each individual and each subject of desire this means reduction of the others to oneself (to be everything).

To want to be everything—or God—is to want to cancel time, is to want to cancel chance (randomness).

Not to want this is to want time and chance.

To want chance is *amor fati* (love of fate).

Amor fati signifies wanting chance, signifies differing from what was.

To attain the unknown and risk it, to gamble it.

For a single entity, to risk stakes is to risk losing or winning. For a totality, it means exceeding the given or going beyond.

In a definitive way, to risk is to bring what didn't exist into being (which is why time is history).

In the union of bodies—in the case of exceeding pleasure—there is a holding onto the suspended moment of ecstatic excitement, of inner surprise, of excess purity. At this moment, existence arises like a bird pursued in the hunt, all in a rush, surging to the heights of the sky. At the same time, though, it's annihilated, taking pleasure in this annihilation from high up, looking out on things with a feeling of strangeness. Exceeding pleasure is canceled, makes way for an annihilating elevation in the bosom of full light. Or rather, as pleasure ceases to be the response to the individual's desire and excessively exceeds this desire, it simultaneously exceeds individual being and replaces it with a shifting—a kind of radiant, excessive suspense connected with a feeling of nakedness and entering into the open nakedness of the other person. Such a state assumes nakedness as being present, as being absolutely there, and it does this by way of an innocent if skillful contact—although the skill I refer to doesn't belong to hands or bodies. It seeks intimate knowledge of nakedness—knowledge of the wound of physical being—whose opening deepens with each contact.

An image of K, from out of nowhere: K as trapeze artist in some music hall. This sort of image pleases her with its logical equilibrium, and together we laugh. I see her suspended under the bright lights, wearing golden spangles.

A young cyclist in the forest wearing his hooded sweatshirt—he's several yards ahead, singing. His voice solemn. In his exuberance his round curly head sways and I notice his full lips as he goes past. The sky's gray, the forest seems bleak—it's cold out. The young man's song gets replaced by continuous foreboding bomber noises—though a little further on, sunlight crosses the road (I'm writing on the hillside, standing up). The muffled sounds gradually get stronger—then a noise of exploding bombs or anti-aircraft fire. Not that many miles from here, so it seems. Two minutes at most, and then silence again. Once more, emptiness. Grayer—more ominous—than before.

My weakness worries me.

Anguish enters and there's no letup, it's choking me in its viselike grip, and I'm breathless. Trying to escape. Blocked. There is no way to admit what is, to admit what requires giving in, in spite of me, to admit what blocks any way out.

My anguish is replicated by another anguish, and there are two of us now, being pursued by a nonexistent hunter, gun in hand.

Nonexistent?

Ponderous neurotic figures afflict us.
Suggesting other figures—equally ponderous, but true.

Reading a work on Descartes, I have to go back over the same paragraph three, four times. I cannot seem to concentrate—my heart beating, temples of my head throbbing. Presently I'm stretching out as if wounded, felled by a terrible if provisional fate. My gentleness with regard to myself calms me: deep inside the anguish that I am is spitefulness, are private hatreds.

Still alone—the idea I might be loving K out of self-hatred scares me. Burning passions prying apart lips, leaving my mouth dry, enflaming my cheeks: these emotions probably relate to some kind of self-revulsion. I don't like myself, don't like K. This evening, kindled by inhuman difficulties, our shared passion reached fever pitch. No matter what the cost, I must escape myself, I must identify with what for me would be an unlimited image. Though an anguish related to feelings of ambiguity paralyzes K.

Struggling against anguish, against neurosis! (Just now, an ear-splitting siren. For me, this listening to a distant rumble of planes becomes the sign of a *morbid*, unhealthy fear). Nothing depresses me any more: six years ago, the neurosis dogging me took my life. In desperation I struggled and felt no anguish, and I thought life was stronger. At first life prevailed. Though neurosis staged a comeback. And death came to my existence.

I have a loathing for oppression and constraints. When, as is the case today, constraint reaches those whose only meaning is to be free—for me, being alongside that kind of constraint is breathing the air of summits—and the loathing I experience is inconceivably great . . .

Constraint is the edge of the past conflicting with what still lives.
Neurosis is the past hating the present—it's relegating the sounds of the human voice to dead people.

From hidden recesses of disaster inside us comes easy laughter, requiring angelic courage.

"The greatness of humankind lies in being a bridge, not a goal—humanness loved for its nature as transition, as decline."
"I love those who lead life in order to founder, to go down—for they will go beyond."
"I love the great ridiculers because they are the great adorers, the arrows of desire ready to fly to the other shore."

If you read them, these sayings of Zarathustra (prologue to the first part) mean little. They suggest possibilities, want to be lived uncompromisingly, unstintingly, by risk takers, by those who regard themselves only as leaps, in which they pass beyond the limits.

Neurosis brings me to a halt—as it does it forces me beyond myself under a threat of going under. Hence the humanness in neurosis, as transfigured in myth, poetry, and drama. Neurosis makes us heroes and saints when not making us invalids. In heroism or holiness, the element of neurosis represents the past, intervening like a limit (constraint) within which life becomes "impossible." Having been weighed down by the past, morbid attachment to which prevents easy access to the present, you can no longer reach the present following familiar paths. This is how the past escapes—while those who are less driven will allow a past to guide or limit them. The neurotic has only a single way out and must risk himself. Life within comes to a halt. Such life can no longer go on along familiar ways, has to open up a new path, create a new world for itself and others.

Childbirth doesn't take place in a day. And many a path is a shining dead-end, though it looks like chance. Paths like these escape the past insofar as they evoke some beyond—though the beyond that is evoked remains inaccessible.

The rule in this area is indefiniteness. There's no knowing if we'll ever get there ("humankind is a bridge, not a goal"). *Maybe* the superman is the goal. But only as evocation, since the superman, if real, would have to risk himself and desire the beyond of himself.

Can't I provide anguish a solution to itself by my taking risks, by becoming a hero of chance? Or rather—freedom? Chance in us takes form as time (loathing the past). Time is freedom. Despite the constraints that fear erects against it. To be a bridge but never a goal—this requires tearing your life away from the norms with an unbending, tightly gripped willpower—a will that will finally refuse to turn away from any dreams.

Time is chance insofar as requiring the individual, the separate being.

It's for and in this individual that a form is new.

Time without risk would be more or less nonexistent. Time wants uniformity dissolved. Without which it would be as if time didn't exist.

Necessarily, for the individual variability is either auspicious or inauspicious, indifferently. The indifference is like not existing. Mischance and chance are arranged in endless permutations as the variability of chance or mischance, with variability being essentially chance (even as it keeps an eye on mischance) and mischance being a triumph of uniformity (including chance's uniformity). Uniform chances and varying mischances indicate possibilities of a tableau in which variation/mischance takes on a tragic attraction (attraction or chance—providing that there's a distance between spectator and spectacle, the spectator taking pleasure in witnessing the collapse, since what sense would there be in the hero dying unobserved?).

(I write on the counter of a bar. During the air raid, drinking—five liqueurs. Tiny, numerous swarms of airplanes sweeping the sky— fierce anti-aircraft fire breaking out. A good-looking girl and her handsome boyfriend dancing—she, half-naked under her beach robe.)

II

FOLLOWING YESTERDAY'S bombardments, communications with Paris are cut off, so it seems. Is this some sudden mischance (from the fact of unfavorable coincidences) following on extreme chance?

For the time being, simply a threat.

At present bad luck reaches me *from all directions.*

I have no recourse. The possibilities that generally people cling to, these, slowly, I let go of.

If there still was time—but instead . . .

Such depression as we walked along the road at afternoon's end! Rain coming down in buckets. For a while finding shelter under a beechtree, sitting on a hill, feet propped on the log. Under lowering skies—the thunder rolling on—as if there'd never be a letup.

In each thing, and in each thing after the next, I'm up against the void. Often my willpower strained, until I allowed it to take over from me—like opening the windows of a house, letting in ruin, wind, and rain. Anguish picked through my obstinacy, and the life that was still in me and sorted them out. The void and nonsense in things—possibilities of suffering, laughter, infinite ecstasy, things as they are as they relate to us, food, drink, the flesh, and beyond the void, nonsense. Despite what I do (or make others do) or speak. Except for babbling on, except for simply asserting that this is how things *are.*

This vulnerable state of laughter, to which I was reduced by struggle, was open to still more struggle.

Fatigue withdraws us from risk taking but struggle doesn't, since in the end struggle contests the value of the state to which we are reduced. This last movement may finally be a wasted cruelty. Though possibly it proceeds from chance. Chance, when occurring, struggles with contestation, contests struggle.

Contesting, questioning, and risking value seem the same. Doubt successively destroys any value whose essence is unchangeable (God or goodness). Risking, however, takes risking for granted as a value. In the process of risking, value is simply displaced from the object to the risking and to the contestation itself.

Questioning replaces unchanging values with a changing value—risking. Nothing in risk taking opposes chance. And were contestation to say, "Whatever is simply chance can't be value, because it isn't unchangeable," it would illegitimately make use of the principle related to what it contests. What's called chance is the value of a given situation, variable in itself. A particular chance is a response to desire. Desire is given in advance, at least as possible desire, even if it isn't evident to begin with.

Moreover I'm unreasonable . . .

. . . and from time to time ridiculously nervous (my endlessly challenged nerves sometimes give way—and do not do a half-bad job of it when they do).

My misfortune is to be—or more exactly to have been—the possessor of such a perfect chance I couldn't have been blessed with a better one, and this chance is yet truer for being fragile and for being gambled at each moment. An utterly overwhelming chance: a chance that lacerates, finally torments me in excesses of joy, fully effecting a happiness whose essence lies in not being comprehended.

Though desire is also present—as is anguish that wants to understand.

The day is coming, with mischance as my guide, when I'll let go of myself for a brief moment—when I'll surrender.

It all seems to be working out. Sometimes tired of waiting, I desire death, and death seems better to me than the state of suspense. I've lost any courage to live, and in my desire for rest, I'm not disturbed by my intuition that the price I would pay would be death.

The happiness I am expecting, as I well know, isn't one that's guaranteed chance, but naked chance—a chance that persists in being free, proudly confined to infinite randomness. How not to gnash our teeth at the idea that horror (perhaps) will turn into unspeakable joy—though death is its only outcome?

What keeps me anguished, I suspect, is a disaster that, in any case, soon will reach me. I see myself slowly but surely arriving at the summit of laceration.

What I can't deny: on my own, I've gone out to greet this impossibility (often we're guided by obscure attractions). What was beneath contempt for me wasn't the fact of being lacerated, but of relinquishing my love, failing to want more risk. Sometimes I'm tempted to hasten the moment of supreme misfortune. It may be I'll stop dealing with my life—but I won't regret having lived it this way.

There is great appeal for me in these words carved in ice by a dying explorer, "No regrets that I came."

For me, once chance is wasted, the idea of reclaiming it (through skill or patience) is a fault—is sinning against chance. Better to die . . .

The return of chance can't come from effort, much less merit. At most, occurring when taking a different viewpoint on anxiety, from favorably noncommittal attitudes, like those of gamblers whom nothing fazes (alongside a suicide's body, I picture a cool, calm, collected gambler, recklessly pouring out his substance).

If chance returns, it's often while I'm laughing at it. Chance is the god whom we blaspheme when something prevents us from laughing at him.

It seemed everything was decided.
Then the wave of planes, the siren . . .
Not worth paying attention to, obviously. But once again—all bets are off.

Sitting down to write, I heard the sound of the all-clear . . .

III

A certain emperor would think constantly of the instability of all things, not to attach too much importance, and to stay calm. Instability has a very different effect on me, and things seem infinitely more valuable to me on account of imperma- nence. It seems to me the most valuable vices, most exquisite balms, have always been tossed into the sea.

—1881–82

SUDDENLY, CLEAR sky . . .
soon covered with black clouds.

Few books have given me as much pleasure as *The Sun Also Rises*.
A sort of resemblance between K and Brett worries me at the same time that it pleases me.
Rereading the fiesta section, my tears overcame me.
Still, there's something missing in the book's abhorrence of intel- lectual forms. I'd rather *throw up*, since dietary abstinence doesn't much appeal to me.

This morning, a harsh sky.
My eyes see—or rather, lacerate—it.
That ancient cloud-being and I know each other—we gauge each other, we even enter each other's bones.
As a result, interpenetrating each other—going deeply, much too deeply into the other—we turn into thin air, annihilating each other. Only emptiness is left, nothingness that resembles the whites of the eyes.

Now as I write a girl comes along, pretty, destitute, healthy, frail. I imagine her naked, I think of going into her—further than herself.

The pleasure I imagine—without *desiring* it in any way—is fraught with a truth that empties out all possibility, spills over the limits of lovemaking. So that only a full and complete sensuality—a full nakedness desiring to be what it is—can slip beyond any possible space.

The necessity for mental strength that lightheartedly goes beyond (erotic) pleasure. Without needing to linger there.

The furthest possibilities in no way cancel the nearest. It's important not to confuse the former with the latter.

In the play of bodies, escaping beyond existence demands that, as existences, we slowly sink to destruction, grapple with each other, and lose ourselves in mutual excesses as we continue onward, slowly attaining the final step beyond possibility. This requires that existence be utterly exhausted—and that rules out anguish (haste). It demands taut power and continuing self-restraint exercised at the exact moment of pitiless descent into destruction and emptiness, whose limits retreat forever. It asks of us a judicious and impassive will power, a rock-hard resolve that slowly rebuffs and defeats difficulties and resistances experienced in laying bare not just others, but ourselves. It demands specific knowledge of the mode wherein the gods desire us to love them: knife of horror in hand. In that senseless direction how difficult to take but a step! At each moment the necessary ecstasies and cruelties exceed the goal. Every stage of the lengthy journey appears interchangeable with every other, continuously—and, if the procedure seems tragic, then soon the feeling of farce makes itself felt, a feeling that has specifically to do with the limits of existence. If it seems comic, the tragic essence escapes, and the individual becomes foreign to the pleasure he or she feels (in a sense, the pleasure is outside—we're robbed, and the pleasure slips through our fingers). The combination of exceeding love and the desire to lose (actually the continuous state of this loss) IS TIME AND IS CHANCE—though this obviously represents a rather rare situation. The individual is the mode in which time occurs. But if the individual has no luck (if chance occurs in the wrong way), that person becomes simply a barrier that obstructs time—becomes simply anguish—or an annulling in which anguish is voided. If anguish is annulled, the individual is finished, having escaped from every occurrence, confined now to extratemporal perspectives. If on the other hand the anguish continues, like Proust in the last volume, the individual has to *rediscover time*. Time—or agreement with time. For each given person, chance is "communication" and loss into another person. "Communication" is the "continuity of that loss." Will I manage to discover the lighthearted, somewhat deranged (subtly analytical) tone of voice that lets me tell the story of the dance around time (*Thus Spake Zarathustra* and *Remembrance of Things Past*)?

Mean-spirited, persistent as a fly, I persistently note, "There is no wall between eroticism and mysticism!"

It's really quite funny—since they use the same words, deal in identical images, and they refuse to recognize it!

Abhorring bodily pollutions, face distorted with hatred, mysticism hypostatizes the fear that contorts it. This fear is the positive object engendered by and perceived in the movement it calls God. Appropriately, the weight of this operation rests on disgust. Located at a juncture point, he's the abyss, on the one hand (uncleanness, a horrible glimpse into the seething powers of the abyss—time . . .) and, on the other, a massive negation sealed off from the abyss (sealed off like pavement—tragically, embarrassedly, sealed off). God! We are still compelled to force human thought into that yawping, needy appeal . . .

> *"If only you were a mystical monk*
> *You would see God!"*

An unchangeable being—which the movement I am referring to represents as definitive—a being never risked, never to be risked in any gambling, in any risking.

Pathetic creatures on their knees . . .

Tirelessly, naively repeating,

"Don't take *our* word for it! Alas, we're not all that logical. We say God—though in reality God is a person, a particular individual. We speak to him. We address him by name—he is the God of Abraham and Jacob. We treat him just like anybody else, like a personal being . . ."

"So he's a whore?"

"   "

Human naïveté—and the obtuse depths of human intelligence—allow every kind of tragic mistake and glaring trickery. Just like sewing a bull pizzle on a bloodless saint, you wouldn't have any hesitation about questioning . . . the immutable absolute! God ripping apart the night of the universe with his screams (Jesus's *Eloi Eloi lamma sabachtani?*)—isn't that the summit of spitefulness? God himself crying out to God with the words, "Why have you forsaken me?" Which is to say, "Why have I forsaken myself?" Or more specifically, "Is this really happening?" And, "Could I have forgotten myself . . . to the point of risking myself?"

On the night of his crucifixion, God, bloody meat, like the nasty secret place in a woman, is the abyss whose negation he is.

I'm not blaspheming. Just the opposite. I've brought myself to the verge of tears—and I'm laughing . . . even as I mix with the crowd . . . laughing at my evocation of time's laceration, in the depths of immutability! For the necessity incumbent upon immutability . . . ? is to change!

Strange that in the mind of the populace . . . God is so quick to untangle himself from the absolute and immutable.

What could be funnier . . . to the point of being crazily profound?

Jehovah untangling himself, nailing himself to a cross!

Allah untangling himself in a game of bloody conquests . . .

Of such divine ways to risk the self, the first gives an idea of comical infinity.

Proust responded—unwittingly, I believe—to the notion of uniting Dionysus and Apollo. The bacchic element is all the more divinely—and cynically—laid bare in the writing, because the work partakes of an Apollonian gentleness.

And isn't the minor modality—as far as it is expressly intended—a mark of divine discretion?

Somewhere between sublime Christian comedy and our joyous drama Blake has left some chance lines.

"On the other hand we want to be the beneficiaries of contemplation and Christian insight . . ." (*The Will to Power*)

". . . to go beyond all of Christianity through Hyperchristianity and not remain satisfied with merely throwing it out . . ." (*The Will to Power*)

"We are no longer Christians and we have gone beyond Christianity, not because we live too far from it but because we are too close, and more particularly because it was our starting point; our simultaneously more demanding and more sensitive devotion bars us from still being Christians today." (*The Will to Power*)

IV

When we use the word "happiness" as defined by our philoso-
phy, we're not in the first place like tired, anxious, world-
weary philosophers, thinking of inner and outer peace in the
absence of pain or the impossibility of tranquility or the
"holiest of holy days" or a stage of equilibrium or something
more or less having the value of deep and dreamless sleep.
Our world rather is an uncertain thing, changing, variable,
equivocal, a dangerous world perhaps, certainly more dan-
gerous than simplicity, immutability, predictability, or
fixity—everything that the earlier philosophers, heirs of the
needs and the fears of the herd, especially honored.

—1885–86

T HE WORLD gives birth and, like a woman, it isn't a pretty sight.

Each roll of the dice is isolated from every other one. Nothing brings them together as a whole. The whole is necessity. The dice are free.

Time makes "what is" occur in individuals.

The individual—in time—is lost, falls into a movement in which he or she is dissolved, is "communication," though not necessarily each with the other.

With this exception: that chance is the individual's duration in his or her ruin. And time, by willing this individual, is essentially the death of that individual (chance is an interference, or series of inter-ferences, between death and existence).

However I might approach the subject, the feeling I have is an awareness of dispersion, of humiliating confusion. I write a book—

and the supposition is, I'll put down ideas in order. To me, delving into particulars while working on a project lessens me. Discursive thought always implies that attention is paid to some single point at the expense of others, pulling us up out of ourselves, reducing us to a link in the chain that we are.

For the "individual as entirety" or the individual who has experienced *impalement*: the fatality of not being fully possessed of his or her intellectual resources. The fatality of work done in a slipshod or messy way.

We live under a threat, since the *function* we employ tends to supplant us! This function can't be employed in excess. We escape the danger only by overlooking it. Work done in a slipshod or messy way—often—is the sole means of not becoming a function.

The opposite danger is as great, though (vagueness, imprecision, mysticism).

The notion of ebb and flow.

There's a deficiency we have to admit here.

"We do not have the right to wish for a single state. We have to desire *to become periodic beings*: like existence." (*The Will to Power*)

In the sunlight this morning, a magical feeling of happiness. The thickness in me now gone—even jubilation no longer an issue for me. An infinitely simple life, blending with the stones, the moss, the sun-filled air.

What I used to think was that the times of anguish (of mishap) prepared the way for the opposite moments—the end of anguish, luminous relief! That's true. Though in the feelings I have this morning—knowing and loving whatever's alive, on the streets, men, children, women—chance and happiness are situated much closer than the most recent leap.

Regarding chance and happiness (coming unexpectedly and calmly, they don't lift me into exaltation): I understood them as gently radiating from simple abundance. There's something offensive in crying out from pleasure. And regarding laughter I've said, "I follow it right to the explosion point. Such is laughter's superfluity, its unfoundedness."

In the woods as the sun came up, I was free, my life rising effortlessly and like a bird in flight, moving through the air—although infinitely free, dissolved and free.

There's so much pleasure in piercing through thickness, seeing into the essence of things, the immense and infinite comedy caused by endless chance, such that it . . . (this is the lacerating, the heart-breaking aspect). Essence? For me. And which figure would be the calm one? It could only be reassuring on condition that I'm uneasiness itself, death itself: an anguish so pure that anguish disappears and a death so perfect that, compared to it, death is just child's play? Would it be me, this figure?

Enigmatic, forcing impossibility to flash outward like soundless lightning, demanding splendid explosions of self, this sense of majesty, more and more shaken with demented laughter . . . so that I'm dying of it.

And this death is not just mine. We are all always dying. The brief movement of time that keeps us from the void is dreamy incoherence. As we leap, it's not so much perhaps that we're flung out among the dead—whom we imagine as being far from us—as that we're hurled beyond. The woman I embrace is dying, and this infinite destruction of individual existences, incessantly flowing, incessantly escaping beyond them, is ME!

V

F OR THE time being, like a fish out of water. Feelings of stifling uneasiness. The mechanism of things grinding to a halt, as I look on. The only way out: impossibility . . .

I'm still awaiting a celebration. Which would be a solution.

Only a moment ago these words from *Gay Science* lacerated me apart—". . . always ready for extremity as I am for celebration . . ." Exhausted, I read of *celebration* in the past . . . (What can I say of the weaknesses and wrong turns of the "morning after the night before," of the time following celebration?)

Yesterday. River flowing gray, under skies thick with wind, dark clouds, dense mists, magic of the whole world suspended in still emerging evening coolness, at the ungraspable moment of inevitable heavy downpour, forests, grasslands trembling in anguish like women about to give in. I'm coming close to the laceration of reason—and within me happiness grows, and with it a growth in my evident inability to possess it! We were like a meadow about to be drenched by rain—vulnerable under wan skies. We had only one choice—to lift our glasses to our lips, drink gently of the immense gentleness of the turbulence of things.

Only a choice for celebration allows life to be lived in time. Can calm happiness go on forever? Redemptive strength can be found only in explosive (and eternal?) joyousness. Its only purpose is to spare us—and the dust particles that we are—a time of decline and anguish—as we proceed inexorably from an explosion to death!

Everyone should understand this and share in the following disclosure:

137

Moralities, religions of compromise, hypertrophies of intelligence, all arise from the sadness that follows the time of celebration. We had to put aside excitement, settle down, and overcome anguish (feelings of sin and bitterness, ashes left in the wake of celebration).

I'm describing "the morning after the night before . . ."

A tiny succulent suddenly recalls the Catalonian farm—hidden away in a distant valley—the one I reached after a long walk in the forest. In the bright sunshine of a quiet uneventful afternoon, the outsize entrance in a state of disrepair—planters containing aloe stood atop the gateposts. The magic mystery of life is suspended—remembering these buildings erected in that remoteness, set up in solitude, for youth, lovemaking, work, celebration, old age, quarreling, death . . .

I'm thinking of this (truer) figure of myself: a man imposing peaceful silence on others—through an excessively sovereign temperament. Solid as the ground, impermanent as clouds. Rising over his own anguish in weightless and inhuman laughter.

The figure of humankind has increased through bold initiatives—and in no way is it my doing that human pride across time is not reflected in my consciousness.

Like a storm over a hollow area, calm will arises above the void. Will assumes the giddying abyss of time—which opens infinitely on nothingness. Will is clearly aware of the pit, in the same movement encompassing dimensions of horror and attraction (the one increasing with the other). Will resists attraction, bars possibility, and in this regard, can even be described as the sign of prohibition. But from its depths, at the same time it draws forth tragic serenity. Action that arises from will cancels time's nothingness and no longer grasps things in their unchanging positions, but in a movement that changes them, in and through time. Action cancels, neutralizes life—but the great moment that says "I will" and commands action is situated on a summit on which can be discerned ruins (or the resulting nothingness) as clearly as the goal (the object changed by action). As will decides to take action, it considers two aspects—the first a destructive nothingness, the second a creation.

As the will views what lies before it (as it elevates the individual who wills and so establishes that person as a splendid, serious, even stormy and rather beetle-browed figure), in relation to the action that it commands, it is transcendent. And the converse, since God's transcendence participates in the movement of will. Generally speaking, whether placing humankind opposite action (opposite the agent as its object) or God opposite humankind, transcendence is imperative by choice.

Strange as it might seem, *pain is so uncommon* we have to look to art so as *not to lack it*. We wouldn't put up with it as it occurred, unless it took us utterly by surprise, as something unfamiliar. But especially, an awareness of nothingness is required—and this is disclosed only by coming to terms with it. The most ordinary events of life suspend us over the abyss. And if we don't encounter the abyss in the unsolicited sufferings coming to us, there are artificial ones, available through reading or in plays—or if we're talented, when we create them. Nietzsche, like others, first and foremost was someone who evoked nothingness by writing *The Origin of Tragedy* (and the nothingness of suffering came to him so he no longer had to strive for it). This privileged state—shared by Proust a little later—is the only one that, *if accepted*, allows us to dispense with transcendence from the outside. True, it understates things to say, *if we accept it*. We have to go further: *if we love it*, if we have the strength to love it. Nietzsche's matter-of-fact relationship to the worst eventualities, his ease and playfulness, these came from the passive presence of the abyss within him. Hence the absence of heavy and constraining raptures that, in mystics, sometimes bring about terrified (thus also terrifying) feelings.

At least the idea of *eternal return* is added . . .

In a spontaneous movement (so it seems), it adds the expansion of eternal time to passive terrors.

But isn't this odd idea simply the price of acceptance, of submission? Or better—of lovemaking? A price, or proof, that has to be provided without any holding back? Hence Nietzsche fell into a swoon as soon as the idea came to him (he describes this in his letters) . . . ?

The idea of return is not immediately effective. By itself it doesn't give a sensation of horror. It might amplify such a feeling if it already existed, but if that sensation doesn't exist it won't arouse additional ecstasy. The reason for this being that somehow or other before entering mystical states we have to be open to the abyss, to nothingness. In every faith the masters of mental prayer urge us to come to this on our own. We ourselves have to make an *effort*. While with Nietzsche, sickness and the way of life it entailed had already done their work. In him infinite echoes of the *return* had a single meaning—infinite acceptance of the fact of horror—and more than infinite acceptance, acceptance preceded by no effort.

The absence of effort!

The raptures of Nietzsche described . . . lighthearted feelings of alleviation, impulses of demented freedom, the pranksterish mood inherent in "extremely elevated states" . . . Is such blasphemous immanence a gift given by suffering?

How lovely *in its weightlessness* is the denial of transcendence and how lovely the denial of its fearsome commandments!

This same absence of effort preceded by the same pain (the same undermining and isolating pain) is found in the life of Proust—each equally necessary to reach states that he reaches.

In Zen *satori* is addressed only through comic subtleties, since it is the pure immanence of the return to self. In place of transcendence—and in the utterly deranged and completely empty abyss—ecstasy discloses the identity of reality and ecstasy, identifying the absurd object with the absurd subject and the time-object that destroys by being destroyed with the subject that is destroyed. In a sense, the reality of this identity is situated at a greater distance than any transcendent reality. It is, it appears to me, the most distant possibility.

I don't imagine attaining satori without first being overwhelmed by suffering.

Satori is attained only effortlessly: and *the smallest thing* provokes it unexpectedly *from the outside.*

The same passivity and absence of effort—and an erosion that is suffering—belong to the *theopathic state*, in which divine transcendence is dissolved. In the theopathic state the worshipper is himself/herself God, and the rapture in which this identification with God is experienced is a simple and "uncomplicated" state, although, like satori, it is situated beyond conceivable rapture.

I once described (*Inner Experience*) the ecstatic experience of the meaning of nonmeaning again becoming the nonmeaning of meaning and then again . . . with no possible outcome . . .

Taking a closer look at Zen methods, you will find that they imply this movement. Satori is sought via concrete nonmeaning substituted for the sensed reality, as revelatory of deeper reality. This is the method of laughter . . .

The subtlety of movement of the "meaning of nonmeaning" is comprehensible in the suspended state depicted by Proust.

A low intensity—and the absence of anything at all remarkable—relate to simplicity of the theopathic kind.

I wasn't familiar with experiences related to the theopathic sort of mystical states known to Proust, when (in 1942) I attempted to work out their nature in *Inner Experience*. At that time I had myself only just come to certain states of laceration. It was only recently that I slipped into theopathy. Immediately I thought of the simplicity of the new state known to Zen, to Proust, and (in a final phase) to St. Teresa and St. John of the Cross.

In the state of immanence—or the theopathic state—falling into nothingness isn't required. The mind itself is wholly steeped in nothingness, it identifies with nothingness (meaning is identified with nonmeaning). The object meanwhile is dissolved into identification with the mind. Time absorbs everything. Transcendence no longer grows at the expense of, or above, nothingness while hating it.

In the first part of this diary I tried to describe that state—a state that eludes the slightest attempt, on the part of aesthetic description, to grasp or comprehend it.

It seems to me that moments of simplicity connect Nietzsche's "states" with immanence. True, these states participate in excessiveness. However, simple, playful times cannot be separated from them.*

*See appendix 2, "Nietzsche's Inner Experience."

VI

It's NOW time to finish this book. In a sense, it's an easy task! I'm aware of escaping countless threats, of slowly getting around them. It wasn't my idea to take up principles as weapons. But in resorting to ruse and calculation . . . and boldly relying on the play of the dice . . . every day I've gone forward, every day managed without difficulty to deal with whatever obstacles presented themselves. The principles of negation that were set out at the beginning have an internal coherence at most. They depend on randomness. Far from acting as hinderances, they proved of more help than their opposites, principles I could deduce today. Using the subtle resources coming from passion, life, and desire against them, I have more decidedly won out than by relying on the wisdom of making assertions.

The lacerating question of this book . . .

posed by a helplessly wounded man, slowly losing his strength . . .

going the limit, though, silently and effortlessly sensing some possibility—despite accumulated obstacles—slipping through the crack in the wall . . .

"if there is no general interrelation of things in the name of which speaking is possible, how can action be addressed, how can people be made to act, do anything?"

Until our time action depended on transcendence. When the talk turned to action, offstage there would always be clunky chains, rattled by ghosts of nothingness.

I want only chance . . .

which is my goal, my only goal, and my sole means.

How painful it is at times to speak. I *love*, and it's my torment not to
be intuitively understood but to be impelled to find words, words
still dripping with lies, steeped in the bitter residue of the times. It
makes me feel nauseous to add (fearing serious misunderstanding),
"I take myself lightly, not seriously."

I'm so lacking any inclination to write for the unfriendly that, from
the rest, the others, I ask *intuitive* understanding. Only friendly eyes
can see far enough. Only friendship senses the uneasiness emerging
from decisive declarations of truth, firm goals. If I ask a man in the
porter's trade to carry my bags to the station, I don't feel uneasy
giving him whatever information is needed. If I evoke the far off
possible, as in a secret love affair, bringing to bear something fragile
and personal, the words I write sicken me and seem empty to me.
I'm not writing a book to preach. *To me it would seem appropriate to
make deep friendship a condition for understanding me.*

"Self-control—Self-appointed moralists who first and foremost advise the necessity of self-control thus gratify a strange mal-
aise: I mean a constant quandry when dealing with impulses and
natural inclinations—whatever could be called urges. Whether it is
exterior or interior peril we refer to, whether we're dealing with
thoughts, attractions, or stimulations, such easily bothered souls always consider their self-control to be imminently in danger. Unable
to trust instinct or spontaneity, they're always on the defensive—eyes
screwed up, sour, opposing even themselves—self-appointed "pro-
tectors of the fortress": even though all the same, *greatness* isn't
beyond them! But how difficult it is for the others to put up with
them! And how unbearable even to themselves they are—how impoverished, how isolated from the soul's utter and lovely randomness,
from all future *experiences*! For indeed, we must lose ourselves, for a
time, so as to learn about existences that we AREN'T . . ." (*Gay
Science*)

How can we avoid transcendence in the way we are brought up?
Clearly, for millennia, humankind has grown up in transcendence
(taboos). Without transcendence would we have arrived at the stage

where we now are (where humanity now is)? To start with something very ordinary—calls of nature—we lead children to discover the nothingness deriving from such sources; and we construct their life on a curse. So we define the power that arises as separate from excrement, coming to be with no conceivable admixture.

Capitalism dies—or will die, according to Marx—from the consequences of consolidation. Likewise, transcendence has become mortal by consolidating the idea of God. From the death of God—who within himself carries the destiny of transcendence—comes the pointlessness of big words and every sort of solemn exhortation.

Without the development of transcendence—transcendence that founds the imperative temper—human beings would have remained animals.

Though the return to immanence takes place at the elevation at which humanity exists.

It raises humanity to where God was, bringing back to a human level the existence that seemed to overwhelm us.

The state of immanence signifies the negation of nothingness (and thus the negation of transcendence; if I simply deny God, I can't draw the object's immanence from that negation). We come to the negation of nothingness in two ways. The first is passive—suffering—shattering and annihilating us until existence is dissolved. The second is active, the way of consciousness: having a particular interest in nothingness, an interest that, though depraved, is already lucid (in depravity itself and in crime, I discern the surpassing of the limits of being), I can in this way come to a clear awareness of transcendence and at the same time its naive origins.

By "negation of nothingness" I have in mind some equivalent of the Hegelian negation of the negation. I want to speak of having "communication" without first having decadence or crime. Immanence signifies "communication" at that stage, without going down or going up again; and in that case nothingness no longer is the object of the attitude that sets it up. If you prefer, profound suffering spares any recourse to the realms of depravity or sacrifice.

The summit that my passion desired to attain—but that I've seen elude my desire—is a summit that in extreme situations chance reaches, in the guise of unhappiness . . .

Is this chance—since it's misfortune?

Here we have to proceed by switching back and forth and saying, "This isn't misfortune, since it's the summit (which desire defines). If a misfortune is the summit, this misfortune fundamentally is chance. Reciprocally if the summit—passively—is attained by misfortune, this is because it is essentially a thing of chance, occurring outside will or merit."

In the summit, I was drawn—in response to my desire—to surpass the limits of existence. And as my will grew tense, because of the fact that falling (my own falling or the falling of desire's object) is a sign of surpassing, it was expressly intended by me. This was the grandeur of evil, falling, and nothingness—giving positive transcendence and moral commandments their value. Such risking became habitual for me . . .

This is the moment when the individual finds out that he or she has become time (and, to that extent, has been eaten away inside), and when, on account of repeated sufferings and desertions, the movement of time makes him or her a sieve for its flow—so that, opened to immanence, nothing remains in that person to differentiate him or her from the possible object.

Suffering abandons the subject (the *inside* of the particular existence that the person is) to death.

Normally it's the opposite, and we seek out the consequences of time and time's expressions (which are nothingness) in the object. I find nothingness in the object, though then a kind of fear restrains me. Hence, what develops is transcendence like a high cliff from which I look down on nothingness.

VII

---

*If ever breath has come toward me, the breath of creative
breathing and necessity, forcing even chance to dance the
dance of the stars;*

*if ever I laughed at the creative lightning, followed growl-
ing but obedient by the lengthy thunder of action;*

*if ever I played dice with the gods at the divine table of
earth so the earth shook and split throwing out rivers of
flame—for the earth is a divine table, trembling with new
words and the sound of the divine dice . . .*

—*Zarathustra*, "The Seven Seals"

*And what difference does it make to you—you dice throwers!
You still have not learned to gamble and show defiance! Are
we not forever seated here at this table, a gathering of mockers
and gamblers?*

—*Zarathustra*, "On the Superman"

M Y PHYSICAL—AND nervous—fatigue is so great that had I not
discovered simplicity, I suppose, anxiety would have left me breathless and lifeless.

Far from achieving immanence, life's unfortunates often dedicated themselves to a God whose transcendence came from an
intended evocation of nothingness. My life on the other hand proceeds from immanence and its impulses. Yet I advance toward
proud sovereignty, raising high my personal transcendence above
the nothingness of possible decline. Each life is composed of subtle
equilibriums.

147

I used to feel the pull of the seamy side of things—the guillotine, the gutter, prostitutes . . . Evil and decline kept me bright-eyed. There emerged a weighty, dark, anguished feeling in me like a burden lying heavy on the crowd, like something evoked in a guillotine song like "The Widow." I was lacerated by this awareness of the dawn as essentially dependent upon decline, as culminating in the half-lights of religion, linking pornography to orgasm.

At the same time I knew I had to get a grip, had to be tough and proud. Occasionally struck by military glory, which to dull, uncomprehending minds issues from a proud contemplation of nothingness—essentially conniving with the evil whose transcendent negation it is (drawing strength sometimes from appearing to disapprove and sometimes from compromise).

I persisted for some time, tasting the bitter truth of those ill-fated possibilities. I rejected arguments from reason, which is a weighing out of pluses and minuses in us and a calculation of clear interests. Reason itself rejects the desire to exceed limits—limits that don't simply mark off the individual's margins but those of reason itself.

In the second part of this book* I attempt to shed light on that mental state. Schematically, I'm trying to suggest the *devout terror* that I'm thrown into by such a state even now.

(In this regard I think the basic aspect of the *will to power* is overlooked if it is not seen as the *love of evil*: not as usefulness, but as a value signifying the summit.)

As to the conclusion of the second part: I affected a certain audacious attitude and challenging tone—no doubt with the same feelings that are in me now.

Even now I can only risk and gamble, without knowing.

(I'm not among those who say, "Do such and thus; and nearly invariably you'll have your results.")

However, by advancing and risking myself—shrewdly, to be sure, if shrewdness was each time a "throw of the dice"—I've changed the way in which I see the difficulties I met with at the outset.

---

*Beginning with part 2, above ("Summit and Decline").

1) When considered in the context of immanence, the summit by definition obviates the difficulties raised regarding mystical states (or at least mystical states that retain, from transcendence, impulses of fear and trembling to which the criticism of "spiritual summits" refers):

—immanence is received and is not the result of searching for it; it is wholly and entirely governed by chance (so that in those areas where intellectual methods are multiplied, clear perspectives can't be given, and if there does exist a decisive moment, it's of secondary importance);

—immanence exists simultaneously and in an indissoluble movement as both an immediate summit (which, from all standpoints, is the same as the individual's destruction) and a spiritual summit.

2) *In risk* I now perceive a movement that, rather than relating the individual's present to his or her future, connects it to *a person who doesn't yet exist*. In this sense risk doesn't assign action to the serving of an agent but serves a still inexistent person. And in this regard it exceeds "being's limits."

In short, although the summit escapes me when I search for it (when I aim at it, as a goal expressed discursively), I can see within me impulses capable of carrying me toward it at any moment. If I can't make the "summit" an object of proceedings or intentions, I can make my life an ongoing evocation of possibilities.

This is how I see things at present:

Time enters me—sometimes by forsaking me to death, a desertion caused by pain acting inside me despite me—though if my life follows its normal course, this will occur through the succession of reflections that attach the smallest actions to time.

To act is to speculate on subsequent results—to sow in hopes of future harvests. In this sense action is "risk," and the "risk" is both the working and the things worked on—such as plowing, a field, grain, or a single part of the possibilities of some individual.

"Speculation," though, differs from "risk," since it is done with a view toward gain. If need be, "risk" can be wild and frantic, independent of concerns for the future.

The difference between speculation and risk comes from different human attitudes.

Sometimes speculation takes precedence over risk. Then the risk is reduced as much as possible, and the maximum possible is done to assure gain—the nature if not quantity of which being limited.

Sometimes the love of risk encourages the greatest risk and results in a refusal to recognize the end being pursued. In this case the end can't be determined: it is by nature an unlimited possibility.

In the first case, speculation on the future subordinates the present to the past. I relate my activity to the being to come, but the limit of this being is wholly determined in the past. The being I am talking about is closed off, intends to be unchangeable—it limits its interests.

In the second case the undefined goal is openness, the surpassing of individual limits: The goal of present activity is the unknown future. The dice are thrown with a view to the beyond of individual being—to what doesn't yet exist. This action exceeds the individual being's limits.

Speaking of summit and decline, I contrasted concern with the future with a concern for the summit, which is located in present time.

I presented the summit as unavailable. In fact, strange as it may seem, the present is always unavailable to thinking. Thought and language have no interest in the present—and at every moment substitute perspectives on a future.

What I said about sensuality and crime can't be changed. If we surpass what I said, it's a principle for us. It's the Dionysian heart of things—to which, once transcendence is dead, pain will cling ever more closely, every day.

All the same I grasped the possibility of action and—in action—of no longer being dependent on the poignant desire for evil.

Strictly speaking, Nietzsche's doctrine remains an appeal with no answer. Rather it's a sickness, since it encourages short-term misunderstandings. The absence of any fundamental goal in this doctrine and its inherent aversion to any goals can't be directly surpassed.

"We believe that humanity's growth has troubling aspects too, and *the greatest humanness that there can be*, if this notion is viable, would be the one that most vigorously represents in itself the contradictions of its existence, glorying in this existence and remaining its sole justification . . ." (*The Will to Power*)

In the absence of goals, ambiguity won't put things right but will end up ruining them. The *will to power* remains equivocal. In a sense, in it is the will to evil, amounting to the will to *expenditure* or risk (which Nietzsche stressed). Anticipations of some human type—related to eulogizing the Borgias—contradict the risk principle, which demands the free occurrence of results.

If I refuse to limit my ends, I act without relating my acts to the good—and without preserving or enriching given beings. To aim at the beyond, and not at a givenness of beings, signifies not closing up but leaving open all possibility.

"It's in our nature to create supermen. *To create what surpasses us!* This is the reproductive instinct, the instinct for action and work. Because a will always supposes some end, humanity *assumes an existence* that is not yet in existence but one that's the end of our existence. That's the real meaning of free will! In this end are summed up love, respect, and glimpses of perfection and ardent hopes." (*The Will to Power*).

In his ideas on children, Nietzsche expressed the principle of open-ended play* *where occurrence exceeds the given*. "Why," said Zarathustra, "should the lion become a child?" A child is innocence and forgetfulness, a new beginning and game, a wheel turning on itself, a first impulse, the sacred "yes."

---

*"Risk," "gambling," "game," and "play" all translate Bataille's *jeu*—TRANS.

The *will to power* is the lion: but isn't the child the *will to chance?*

When still young, Nietzsche noted: " 'Play' or uselessness—the ideal of exuberant strength and childlike qualities. This is God's 'infantilism.' " (*The Will to Power*)

Apparently the Hindu Ramakrishna attained to the condition of immanence. He said of God, "He's my playmate." And, "There's no rhyme or reason to the universe. It's sheer playfulness—tears and smiles, characters in a play. Oh! Such entertainment of the world— groups of children let loose—and who's to blame or praise? There's no such thing as an explanation or brains—and we're deceived by the few explanations that exist. But this time I'm not taken in. *My watchword is play.* Beyond reason, knowledge, words of any kind, is love."

I'm thinking—I'm not sure of what—maybe about a type of speaking so successful that, in spite of itself, it deforms the reality it refers to. In the immanent state are united the sense of the tragic, feelings of demented comedy, and the greatest simplicity. Simplicity is the decisive aspect. Immanence hardly differs from any state at all, and specifically it consists in this: that this hardly and this *next to nothing* matter more than anything else you can imagine.

It may be that *play as a watchword* and *love* obscure the truth.

But it's no accident, I imagine, if these few lines establish the equivalence of the object grasped in immanence, in infinite vistas of play.

A state of immanence implies such a wholehearted "risk" of self that only independently occurring willpower can command the individual who gets to such an extreme distance.

Once the lie of transcendence is revealed, responsibility is forever dissipated. In the absence of responsibility, however, the deep infinity inherent in risk escapes as well. Risk is a quest, from occurrence to occurrence, in the infinity of possibles.

In any event.

The state of immanence signifies *beyond good and evil*.

And is related to nonascesis and to the freedom of the senses.

This applies also to the innocence of risk.

Upon reaching immanence, our life has finally left the stage of the masters behind.

August 1944

IF ONE day I broke apart, dividing if not my whole life from the masses, at least the important part of it—if the masses are dissolved in endless immanence—it would only happen at the cost of depleted strength! In the period in which I write, transcending the masses is like spitting in the air: what you spit out falls back on you . . . Transcendence (noble existence, moral disdain, an attitude of sublimity) has declined, becoming hypocrisy. It's still possible to transcend states of apathy, but only on condition of losing ourselves in immanence—and given that we fight for others too. I would feel averse to transcendent impulses (categoric decisions) if I didn't immediately grasp them as canceled in a kind of immanence. What is basic for me is to exist *on the human level* and to transcend only the decline, the plaster decorations of transcendence. If I weren't myself on the level of workers, my transcendence above the workers would amount to a sticky gob of something at the end of my nose. That's how I feel at cafes, in public places . . . I physically judge the people I mix with, and they can't be below or above a certain level. I'm deeply different from the workers. But the feelings of *immanence* I have when talking to them, that is, when we're together in our sympathies, are an indicator of my place in the world—a sign of the wave in the midst of ocean. The bourgeoisie, meantime, secretly jockeying with each other: apparently condemned to empty exteriority.

On one hand, reduced to hypocrisy (the play-acting of pretending to be masters—lords of bygone days—connected with risking death, sword in hand), transcendence produces men whose vulgarity sheds light on deep immanence. Yet I picture the bourgeoisie as destroyed in a few legitimate bloodlettings. Wouldn't the equality of those who were still there then, wouldn't that infinite immanence in its turn make the monotonous reproduction of the workers pointless, wouldn't it render useless a multitude without history or difference?

157

But that is only theory!

In any case, the sense of immanence within the masses (which wouldn't be transcended from then on) relates to needs as necessary for me as physical lovemaking. If, to respond to greater demands such as a desire for gambling, I felt it necessary to isolate myself in a *new* transcendence, I'd be in the wretched condition of people dying.

This afternoon: Four American planes attacking a train loaded with oil and gasoline (the train in a station a mile or so from here), hitting it with bombs, artillery, machine guns. The planes flew low, buzzed roofs, darting through black columns of smoke—like awkward scary insects—dive-bombing the train, then up again to the sky. Every few minutes there would be another one up above us, plunging through thundering machine gun fire, the motors, the bombs, the rapid-action artillery guns. For a quarter of an hour, and without any personal risk, I watched this pageant; it fascinated the viewers. We trembled and marveled—and *after the fact* we thought of the victims. Some thirty train cars burned. And billowing up for hours, as if from a crater, huge smoke clouds darkened parts of the sky. At an aquatic festival two hundred yards from the train, large numbers of children had gathered. No one dead, no one injured.

No further radio reports on the advances of the armored columns. In any case, I'm assuming that they're less than twenty miles from here. A couple of pickup trucks with German troups inside stopped in front of me. Looking for a bridge over the Seine, irregularly fleeing east.

For the first time (regarded from a more or less dispassionate viewpoint, however) I've grasped the meaning of the war, that it is a transcendence against immanence. The defeat of National Socialism connects with the isolation of transcendence and the Hitlerite illusion—as the latter, in a movement of transcendence, is unleashed in force. Slowly the force mobilizes a greater force against it—the result of reactions realized within immanence. What alone is left is the limit of isolation.

In other words: if the essence of Fascism is national transcendence, it can't become "universal." It draws its particular force from "particularity." Which is why it loses the cause it represented, though it had universal aspects. In each country, a certain number wanted control over the masses, taking personal transcendence as their goal. They were frustrated seeking it, on account of not being able to offer the masses the option of following them in this movement—and so thereby transcending the rest of the world. That was possible only in a single country, in the transcendence of its satellite (Italy)—which turned out to be comical by the middle of the war (the war hasn't demonstrated that Italian Fascism is basically inferior compared to the German type but that, united with and subordinate to a greater movement, the German kind eclipses the Italian).

It is also funny for me to be playing "owl of Minerva," speaking only after the fact, greeting war victims with bursts of laughter. Is this clear-headed or cruel laughter? Clear-headed, since immanence is freedom and laughter. "Momentary tragedy," Nietzsche said, "aids the eternal comedy of existence, and the sea 'with its countless smiles'—to quote Aeschylus—will cover the greatest of tragedies with its waves." (*Gay Science*)

I am imagining a split across immanence, each party contesting the other's authenticity and approaching any authenticity only from the fact of contesting and being contested. The tension—if not the war necessary between the two—and the fact that neither is what it claims to be.

Plans for a coherent philosophy—but that's now over and done with . . .
Endless waiting, numerous explosions in the night. The pro-German mayor yesterday announced that the Americans are entering Paris. I doubt it. While I write, a fierce explosion, a child howling. Everyone on pins and needles from waiting. The day before yesterday the Americans came to within a few miles. Discounting any ordinary interests, personally, I have morbid reasons for awaiting the

developments, especially the Americans reaching Paris. Only a slim
likelihood of the region being wracked by major battles. The Germans are leaving.

Only transcendence (discontinuity) is understood. Continuity is
not understood except as related to the opposite. Pure immanence
and the nothingness of immanence equate and signify *nothing*.

Not that a pure transcendence is intelligible either, except when
repeated, and this amounts to saying—except when represented to
infinity in the homogeneous environment of immanence.

With communications cut, I'm thrown back on total solitude. With
the German departure a couple of days ago, a kind of no man's land,
as the phrase goes, has been set up at the edge of the forest—a
perimeter the Americans won't cross. You wouldn't have imagined
emptiness along the road, the nightly silence . . . The planes few and
far between, and sounds of explosions abating. No more bombings—
and no artillery fire to be heard. Whatever is alive, the village
populations, the armies, all are dissolved (exhausted) in expectation.
Since there's no trusting the news, I've stopped making any in-
quiries. Any news I need to know (the Americans reaching Paris or
arriving here) will come to me on its own.

Under these conditions, uncertainty on the subject of K remains
sheer agony: in this remote, sealed-off area it undermines and destroys me.

The relatively slow military operations stir up people's legitimate
fears.

The issue of the fighting in Paris.

I experience relief imagining untold excesses of suffering instead
of an expectedly swift liberation. Sometimes we prefer dealing with
horror to be being patient.

So I am jumpy now—sometimes at least. I pull myself together, and self-control returns through writing. It's getting dark out, and there isn't any electricity, though I'm reluctant to burn candles. I want to write, not give in to anxiety. For months now the separation forced on me by the approaching military operations has been all too obvious. And now I can say of my loneliness that it's oppressive beyond bearing. In this absence, my obsession turns nothingness (which might be definitive) into a test—and it stifles me. It's so utterly exhausting to live out the projection we make of such stifling nothingness, projecting it onto the lie of transcendence! If the torment was pure, if it was an authentic nothingness, it would probably lie less heavily. If I have to die, that's a lie too—though no doubt the lie of losing the beloved is more glaring. But the lie of living, once shown up for what it is, decreases the sadness of dying, while the lie of love increases the horror of losing the beloved. In both cases, the evident character of the lie does away with only a part of the result— since lying has become our truth. What I call lying, what the lie essentially is, is only essentially a lie: it is the impotence of the truth, shall we say. If loss—and not fatigue—presents us with the image of ourselves as working ourselves into a lather over nothing, the feeling of impotence that crushes us becomes nerve-wracking. It can't suppress the attachment. The separation isn't easier for that reason—and detachment doesn't bring about the lucidity we hoped for, but the thought that not even return can satisfy the yearning subsisting at the core of deception.

A feeling of being twenty years younger.

I found a divinely hellish messenger, one right out of musical comedy.

Saw K. We heard the roar of the artillery and the sound of machine guns!

This evening, up in the tower. The huge forest under low rain clouds. The war coming to its limit. From the southwest to the east, dull rumbling.

The coming battle—sounds of which several of us go out to hear standing on boulders—doesn't faze me. Like my neighbors, in the distance I see the spot where the invisible and mysterious battle takes place—though we hear contradictory speculations. The no man's land no longer in force. In front of us scattered Germans slow the American advance. That's it—that's all I know. The radio news is confusing, not squaring with the German resistance we can see opposite us. Knowing little or nothing—artillery and machine-gun noise, smoke clouds from distant fires, all these don't seem at all problematic to us. Awesomeness, whatever its explanation, derives from incomprehensibility. The sounds suggest neither the lethal effects of projectiles, nor the vast canvas of history, nor even the approaching danger.

I feel empty and tired, still cannot write—but not because of the state of my nerves. I need rest and mindless relaxation. I'm reading novels by Hervieu and Marcel Prévost in magazines from the 1890s.

It's most likely that the Germans are giving up. By night, artillery rattles our doors. At the end of the day, there are some twenty incredibly violent explosions (a major munitions depot blows up). I feel the shock waves between my shoulders and legs. A few miles from here flames lick the sky—I see an explosion from atop the boulders. At the skyline, immense blindingly red flames leap through black smoke. The wooded skyline is the same I saw three months ago when I complained of lack of imagination. At the time I couldn't imagine battle lacerations, the devastation of lovely vistas— like immense slow waves moving over oceans of trees. Today I saw huge conflagrations. Five or six miles from here, an artillery spits out its rage, its sounds eventually swallowed by enormous explosions. But on top of the boulders the children are laughing. The calmness of the world remains integral.

Finally the news is less confused. Two cyclists arriving from Paris tell me what's happened—street fighting, a French flag raised over city hall, newsboys hawking *l'Humanité*. According to them, the fighting nears Lieusaint and Melun. Melun might fall this evening. That would decide the fate of the forest.

Went to the boulders at nine this evening. Strong artillery fire, which then goes silent. Though sounds of motorized columns can be heard in the forest.

Got back, stretched out on my bed. Awakened from my half sleep by shouts. Went to the window, saw women and children running and shouting. The Americans are here they say. Going outside, I find tanks surrounded by the crowd—in what might be called a holiday mood, but more excited. It isn't as if these emotions don't touch me as much as anyone. I talk to the soldiers. Joke and laugh a bit.

There is something pleasant about the look of these Americans—their clothes and their gear. Compared to us, the overseas visitors seem more self-contained, more integral.

The Germans in any case exude transcendent mediocrity. The "immanence" of Americans is undeniable (their existence is in themselves and not beyond).

The crowd brought with them flags, flowers, champagne, pears, tomatoes and lifted children onto the tanks not a quarter of a mile from the Germans.

Arriving at noon, the tanks are on their way again by two. Afterward, pitched battle half a mile from the streets. Part of the afternoon spent listening to machine gun onslaughts, the deafening bursts of artillery, the rifle fire. From atop the boulders, I saw the smoke billowing from a bombed-out village, the German battery firing from it. Everywhere I turned—fire! Melun burned in the distance, a volcano belching smoke. From atop the boulders you see the land stretching out, two thirds of it a gently rolling old-growth forest, then a flat part going on toward Melun. Occasional planes at the horizon swooping on a German column, and as they struck, I saw columns of smoke go up.

Nine P.M. Slow arrival of a pickup truck, armed Resistance men surrounding it. Flags deck out the town square where the crowd gathers. The first to be put in the truck is tall and lean, an older man.

He's exotic and distinguished, like a bird, a general. Disgraced—his feet hanging out over the edge—the picture of wariness, disillusion. Surrounded by the armed mob. He bossed local collaborationist forces. The scene seems repulsive—a neighborhood "execution cart" replicating the Revolution, victims withdrawn into a deathly solitude. The crowd cheers the arrival of a woman, they strike up "The Marseillaise." A petite middle class woman (is she forty years old?) starts in on "The Marseillaise" again, and the rest join in. By the looks of her she is mean spirited, narrow-minded. Hearing her sing is disgusting and ridiculous. Arrival of nightfall: a low, black sky indicates a storm. The townspeople bring in the mayor, then come the rest. First there are disagreements regarding the mayor, then a shoving match ensues. The pickup truck with its burden making its way through at a snail's pace. Bare-headed young men armed with rifles or submachine guns climb among the prisoners. The discordant strains of the "Chant du Départ" are heard. In the glare of the fires, night takes on a reddish hue. At times lightning flashes across the sky blindingly—everything madly pulsating. Toward the end, the nearby artillery (troop lines a quarter of a mile away) spews out pitched violence, making this wretched situation that much worse.

I'm frightened by those who find it easy to reduce political activity to propaganda cliches. Personally, the notion of the hatreds, hopes, hypocrisies, stupidities (in short, feints of *interest*) accompanying the great movements of weaponry obliterates me. Conflagrations appearing and disappearing on a battlefield, people charging helter-skelter through the streets, bursts of artillery, and a din of explosions—all seems fraught, in no ordinary way, with the burden associated with the destiny of our species. What unfamiliar reality pursues its end (different from the goals we see) or pursues no end at all through such noise?

Not much keeps us from concluding that the immense convulsion now going on relates necessarily to the destruction of the old order, with its lies, frantic shouts, sophistication, morbid sweetness. On the other hand there is a world of *real* forces aborning, a world acting freely. The past (the deceit required to maintain it in existence) is now dying: Hitler's cumbersome efforts draw on the last of its resources.

In this regard, obviously—woe betide those who won't be here to see the coming of the time for casting off old clothes and going naked in the new world: a world where *what has never been seen before* remains the sole condition of possibility!

But what does this world being born want? What does it seek? And what does it signify?

Lacerated this morning, my wound opening again with the slightest jostling. Once more, empty desire and inexhaustible suffering! A year ago in the heat of my decisiveness I distanced myself from the barest possibility of rest. For a year I've been thrashing about like a fish out of water. I'm eager and laughing, becoming a fiery rush . . . Suddenly: emptiness and absence. And from now on I'm *at the foundation of the world*: from that foundation the fiery rush appears simply betrayal.

How can we help realizing—and then endlessly sensing over and over again—the lie of objects that excite our desire? Yet in this senseless darkness, further than nonsense and collapse, I am still lacerated by a passion to "communicate" the news of a nightfall to my beloved, as if this "communication" alone and no other would suffice as a measure of love's greatness. Thus—endlessly here and there—the mad lightning stoke of chance is reborn, demanding in us, as a prerequisite, the realization of the lies and nonsense that it is.

Oh summit of all that is comic! Bound, as we are, to flee the emptiness (insignificance) of infinite immanence, insanely dedicating ourselves to the lie of transcendence! But in its dementia this lie lights up immanent immensity. An immensity now no longer a pure nonsense or a pure emptiness, *it is* the foundation of full being, a true foundation before which the vanity of transcendence dissipates. We wouldn't ever have known transcendence (*for us* it could not have been—and this may be the only way it can exist *for itself*) if we hadn't first constructed it and then rejected it, torn it down.

(Will you be able to follow me this far?)

And truly, we're guided to that point by a commonly noted light proclaimed by the word FREEDOM.

To which I am deeply attached.

I don't know if anxiety—and inner unrest—ever more cruelly lacerated anyone. At present my place isn't with those who teach. Whatever statement I make continues on in me as in a town hit by bombs, the bombing reverberates in chaos, dust, and moans.

But just as the event being past, the community discovers itself beyond the calamity (cautiously, as tears dry up, as closed faces regain their light, as laughter cavorts again)—in the same way, the "tragedy of reason" changes to senseless variation.

Appendices

APPENDIX I
NIETZSCHE
AND NATIONAL SOCIALISM

Nietzsche attacked idealist morality. He ridiculed kindness and pity, revealed the pretense and unmanliness hidden in humanitarian sentimentalty. Like Proudhon and Marx he insisted on the beneficial side of war. Quite distant from the political parties of his time, he happened to set forth principles for an aristocracy of "masters of the world." He praised beauty and physical force, had a distinct preference for life's risky, turbulent aspects. These straightforward value judgments, distinct from liberal idealism, made the Fascists claim him as one of theirs, led certain anti-Fascists to see him as a Hitler predecessor.

As Nietzsche realized, the near future would see the exceeding of conventional limits opposed to violence and the clashing of real forces in conflicts of outsize proportions, clashes that would violently and materially bring all existing values into question. He pictured the woes of a wartime period that would be of unprecedented harshness, and he didn't believe we should avoid such miseries regardless of cost or that those trials would surpass human strength. To him even catastrophes like this seemed preferable to stagnation, to the lies of bourgeois life, to the banal happiness preached by a herd of professors of morality. In principle, he posed the question of whether authentic value exists for humankind, whether prescriptions of conventional morality and traditional idealism obstruct the coming of that value, and whether life will overturn conventional morality. The

Marxists similarly understand moral prejudices—understanding them as opposed to revolutionary violence and yielding to some sort of preeminent value (the emancipation of the proletariate). Though different from Marxism's value, the value proclaimed by Nietzsche isn't less universal—since the emancipation he wanted wasn't that of a single class relative to others but the freeing of human life under the example of its best representatives—compared to the moral slavery of the past. Nietzsche dreamed of a humanness that, far from fleeing its tragic fate, would love and embrace this fate to the fullest, a humanness that would no longer lie to itself and would raise itself above the social slavishness.

This sort of humankind differs from the present-day kind, which is normally confused with a function that's only part of human possibility. Putting it succinctly, this new humanness would be *integrally human* and freed from the slavery that limits us. Nietzsche had no desire to define such a free and sovereign humankind, halfway between modern humanity and a super-humanity, that is, superman. Appropriately, he thought when something is free, you can't define it. Could anything be more vain than designating or limiting a thing that doesn't yet exist? It's up to us to will it! To will the future is to recognize the known as to be surpassed. With this principle—a primacy of the future over the past* to which he remained loyal—Nietzsche becomes as disconnected as possible from what is despised by life under the name of death, or by dreams under the name of reaction. Between the ideas of Fascist reactionaries and Nietzsche's notions there is more than simple difference—there's radical incompatibility. While declining to limit the future, which has all rights according to him, Nietzsche all the same suggested it through vague and contradictory suggestions. Which led to confusions and misunderstandings. It's wrongheaded to attribute definite intentions to him regarding electoral politics, arguing that he talked of "masters of the world." What he intended was a risked evocation of possibility. As for the sovereign humanity whose brilliance he wanted to shine

---

* A primacy of the future over the past, which is essential to Nietzsche, has nothing to do with the primacy of the future over the present that was mentioned earlier.

forth: in contradictory ways he saw the new humankind sometimes as wealthy, sometimes as poorer than the workers, sometimes as power-ful, sometimes as tracked down by enemies. He required of the new humankind that it possess a capacity to withstand adversity—while recognizing its right to trample on norms. Still, he distinguished this humanity on principle from men in possession of power. He recog-nized no limits, and confined himself to describing as freely as he could the field of a possible.

This said, if "Nietzscheanism" has to be defined, there isn't much reason to dwell on the part of this doctrine that assigns all rights to life as opposed to idealism. A rejection of classical morality is com-mon to Marxism,* Nietzscheanism, and National Socialism. The only essential is the value in whose name life asserts these higher rights. Once this principle of judgment is established, Nietzschean values are seen as opposing racist values within a context of the whole.

—Nietzsche's initial stance develops out of admiration for the Greeks, the most intellectually developed people of all time. In Nietzsche's mind everything is subordinated to culture. While in the Third Reich, a reduced culture has only military might as its end.

—One of the most significant traits of Nietzsche's work is its glorification of Dionysian values, that is, infinite intoxication and enthusiasm. It's no coincidence that Rosenburg's *Myth in the Twentieth Century* denounces the cult of Dionysus as non-Aryan! . . . Despite hastily repressed inclinations, racism admits only military values. "Youth needs stadiums, not sacred groves," asserts Hitler.

—I already talked about the opposition of the past to the future. Strangely enough, Nietzsche designates himself as a child of the future. He himself linked the phrase with the fact of his not having a native land. And actually, our native country is what belongs to the past in us. It's on this and this alone that Hitlerism erects its rigid

---

* Which in terms of morality is located in the aftermath of Hegelianism. Hegel had already distanced himself from tradition. And quite legitimately, Henri Lefebvre said Nietzsche adopted as his own "unconsciously, the task of a sometimes too zealous popularizer of immoral-ism implicit in Hegel's historical dialectic" (H. Lefebvre, *Nietzsche*). To use Lefebvre's termi-nology, Nietzsche is responsible for "pushing through already opened gates."

value system, adding no new value. Nothing could be more alien to Nietzsche, who—against the world—asserts the total vulgarity of the Germans.

—Two official precursors of National Socialism prior to Chamberlain were Nietzsche's contemporaries, Wagner and Lagarde. Nietzsche is appreciated and has been pushed to the forefront in the propaganda effort, but the Third Reich doesn't consider him one of its teachers in the same way it eventually does the other two. Nietzsche was a friend to Richard Wagner but broke off, disgusted by his Francophobic and anti-Semitic chauvinism. As for the pan-Germanist Paul de Lagarde, a single text removes any doubts on that score. "If you only knew," Nietzsche wrote Theodor Fritsch, "how I laughed last spring reading works by a self-important, stubborn sentimentalist by the name of Paul de Lagarde . . ."

—Today of course we're aware how anti-Semitic stupidity functions in Hitlerite racism. There's nothing more essential to Hitlerism than hating Jews. Opposing this is the following rule of conduct of Nietzsche's: "No friendship with anyone implicated in this barefaced hoax of races." Nietzsche asserted nothing more wholeheartedly than his loathing of anti-Semites.

I have to insist on this last point. Nietzsche's fate was to be tarred with the Nazi brush. Certain hypocricies have to be dealt with for that reason. One was perpetrated by the philosopher's own sister who survived him and lived on till very recently (she died in 1935). When November 2, 1933, arrived, Mrs. Elizabeth Foerster, born Nietzsche, could still recall the difficulties that arose between her and her brother—difficulties stemming from her 1885 marriage to the anti-Semite Bernard Foerster.

A letter in which Nietzsche reminds her of his disgust (he refers to it as being *as pronounced as possible*) for the man whom she chose to be her husband (he calls him by name) was published through her efforts. November 2, 1933, in the house where Nietzsche died, Mrs. Elizabeth Judas-Foerster received Adolf Hitler, Fuhrer of the Third Reich. On that solemn occasion she attested to the family's anti-Semitism by reading a text by . . . Bernard Foerster!

"Before leaving Weimar to go to Essen," reported the *Times* on

November 4, 1933, "Chancellor Hitler paid a visit to Mrs. Elizabeth Foerster-Nietzsche, the sister of the celebrated philosopher. The elderly lady made him a gift of a walking stick once belonging to her brother. She invited him to visit the Nietzsche Archives.

"Mr. Hitler listened to her read from a memorandum addressed to Bismarck in 1879 by Dr. Foerster, the anti-Semitic agitator who protested against the incursions of the Jewish spirit in Germany. Taking Nietzsche's walking stick in hand, Mr. Hitler strode through the crowd to great huzzahs."

In 1887, addressing a contemptuous letter to anti-Semite Theodor Fritsch, Nietzsche ended this way, "So then really, what do you think I feel when the name of Zarathustra issues forth from the mouths of anti-Semites?"

APPENDIX II
NIETZSCHE'S INNER EXPERIENCE

The "experiences" adduced here are allotted less space than in the two earlier books.* In addition, they lack the clarity they had there. Nor is this simply the way it appears. Indeed, the essential interest of this book impinges on moral anxieties. But "mystical states" are no less important than they were previously, because the moral question is raised in that context.

It might appear a distortion to give such a role to these states in a book "on Nietzsche." The work of Nietzsche hasn't a lot to do with investigations into mysticism. But Nietzsche did experience some kind of ecstasy and said as much (*Ecce Homo*—see above, p. 93).

I wanted to arrive at an understanding of the "Nietzschean experience." I imagine Nietzsche as having in mind these same "mystical states" in passages in which he speaks of a divine.

"And how many new gods are still possible!" he writes in a note dating from 1888. "As for me, in whom the religious instinct, that is, the instinct to *create* gods, is at times awkward and untutored, how various are the modes in which I have had, each time, some revelation of the divine! . . . I have seen so many strange things occurring during these times outside time, moments that drop into our lap as if out of the skies, times when it becomes less and less clear to what extent you are perhaps already old or will become young again . . ." (*The Will to Power*)

---

* Bataille means *Inner Experience* and *Guilty*—TRANS.

To this text I add two more:

"To see tragic natures founder and *be able to laugh* despite feelings of profound understanding, emotion, and sympathy, which are also felt: this is divine." (*The Will to Power*)

"My earlier solution: take tragic *pleasure* in a vision of the highest and best foundering (a pleasure issuing from an understanding that the highest and best remain too limited with respect to the Whole); though this is only a mystical way of intuiting some higher 'good.'

"My most recent solution: supreme good and supreme evil are identical." (*The Will to Power*)

The object of these "divine states" known to Nietzsche is a tragic content (time), while their dynamic is to reabsorb a transcendent tragic element into an immanence implied by laughter. The "too limited with respect to the Whole" of the second quote refers to this same impulse. "A mystical way of intuiting" means the mystical mode of feeling in the sense of experience, not mystical philosophy. This being the case, the tension of states of extremity is given as a search for a *higher "good."*

The phrase "the supreme good and supreme evil are identical" could also be understood as a fact of experience (the object of ecstasy).

The importance accorded by Nietzsche himself to these extreme states is expressly brought out in this note: "The new feeling of power is the state of mysticism; and the clearest, boldest rationalism is only a help and means toward it.—Philosophy expresses extraordinarily elevated states of soul." (*The Will to Power*). The phrase "elevated states" to designate mystical states is already found in *Gay Science* (see above, p. 91).

Among other things this passage recalls an ambiguity brought home by Nietzsche when he speaks tirelessly of *power* while having in mind the capacity to give. In fact we can only understand another observation (from about the same time) in this same way: "The definition of a mystic: someone with enough happiness of his own, maybe too much, seeking a language for his happiness because he wants to *give away* that happiness" (*The Will to Power*). In that sense Nietzsche defined an impulse from which Zarathustra in part derives. The mystical state, elsewhere identified with power, is more properly seen as the desire to give.

This book has the following profound meaning: that extreme states escape the control of the will (because humanity is action, plans), and this could be conveyed through speech only with an alteration of human nature. The decisive value of that prohibition can only lacerate us when we will and when we speak—and if willing and speaking are what we cannot do, they are precisely what we must do. And regarding me, I have *enough, I have too much, of my own happiness.*

APPENDIX III
INNER EXPERIENCE
AND ZEN

The Zen Buddhist sect existed in China from the time of the sixth century. Today it flourishes in Japan. The Japanese word Zen translates the Sanskrit *dhyana*, designating Buddhist meditation. Like yoga, *dhyana* is a breathing exercise for ecstatic ends. Zen is distinguished from ordinary paths by its evident contempt for gentle procedures. Although the basis of Zen devotion is meditation, its only end is the illuminatory moment known as *satori*. Access to satori doesn't derive from any methods that can be comprehended. It's a sudden dislocation, an abrupt opening unleashed by the unforeseen experience of strangeness.

Sian Jen's master Wei Chan refused to teach him, and he was desperate. "As he was weeding and sweeping the ground one day, a pebble he just then tossed away struck a piece of bamboo; the sound produced by this impact unexpectedly raised his mind to satori. The question Wei Chan posed became luminous; his joy knew no bounds; it was *as if he had found a lost relative*. In addition, he understood how kind his older brother had been, whom he neglected because the latter refused to instruct him. For he knew this would not have happened if Wei Chan had been so bereft of kindness as to proffer explanations to him" (Suzuki, *Essays on Zen Buddhism*). Emphasis on the words "As if he had found . . ." is my own.

"When the release takes place, whatever is born in the mind

explodes like a volcanic eruption or spills out like lightning. Zen calls
this 'return to self' . . ." (Suzuki).

Satori can come about "from hearing an indistinguishable sound or
unintelligible remark, from observing a flower open, from some sort
of trivial everyday incident like falling over, rolling up a mat, using a
fan, etc." (Suzuki).

A monk arrived at satori "while walking in the courtyard, the moment
he stumbled" (Suzuki).
      "Ma Tsu twisted Pai Tchang's nose" . . . and opened his mind
(Suzuki).

Zen expression often took a poetic form. Jang Tai Nien wrote:

> *Should you wish to conceal yourself in the north star,*
> *Turn around, cross your hands behind the south star.*
>   (Suzuki)

SERMONS OF JUN MEN. "One day . . . he said: 'The Bodhisattva
Vasudeva changes for no reason at all to a stick.' So saying, he traced a
line on the ground with his own stick and continued, 'All Buddhas, as
numerous as the grains of sand, are present to speak all manner of
nonsense.' Then he left the room. Another time he said, 'What then
is the point of all the words I have spoken till now? Again, being
incapable of coming to my own aid, I'm here to speak to you once
more. In this immense universe is there anything that stands in your
way and makes you a slave? If ever you find the slightest thing on your
path or obstructing your way, though it's small as a pinpoint, please
remove it! . . . If despite yourselves you let yourselves be taken in by
an old man such as me, you've already lost your way and you'll break
your legs . . .' Another time, 'Observe—there's no such thing as life
that persists!' And so saying he made as if to fall down. Then he
asked, 'Do you understand now? If not, ask this stick for explanations!' " (Suzuki).

APPENDIX IV
REPLY TO JEAN-PAUL SARTRE
(DEFENSE OF *INNER EXPERIENCE*)

The disconcerting element in my writing style lies in the fact that its seriousness is not what it seems. The seriousness isn't intentionally deceptive, but what could keep extreme seriousness from turning into laughter? Unambiguously expressed, excessive mobility of concept and feeling (states of mind) obstructs the slower reader's capacity for grasping (getting a steady hold).

Sartre said about me: ". . . submerged in nonknowing he rejects every concept that permits the designation and classification of what he then reaches: 'If I said decisively, "I saw God," what I see would change. Instead of the inconceivable unknown—wildly free before me and leaving me wild and free before it—there would be the dead object, the object of the theologian.' However, all is not so clear, and here is what he now writes: 'My experience of the divine is so demented "you'd laugh if I told you," ' and further on: 'to me, a fool, God speaks mouth to mouth' . . . Finally, as he begins a curious chapter containing an entire theology, he again explains his refusal to speak the name of God, though in a rather different way: 'What basically deprives humanity of any possibility of speaking of God is the fact that in human thought God necessarily conforms to humanity insofar as humanity is tired and yearning for sleep and peace.'

Reply to a critique of *Inner Experience*, which appeared in *Cahiers du Sud* under the title, "A New Mystic."

Here you will not find the scruples of the agnostic who, between atheism and faith, understands how to stay in suspense. This is the true mystic speaking, the mystic who, having seen God, rejects the all-too-human language of those who have not seen him. In the gap separating these two passages, you will find all of Mr. Bataille's bad faith . . ."

Sartre's opposition here helps me emphasize the essentials. My idea is that the particular human experience called the God experience is altered by naming it. In this respect, a simple representation of the object suffices, since the need for precautions doesn't change the situation. On the contrary, should the name be avoided, the theology dissolves and after that is just a memory—consigning this experience to despair.

Sartre, basing himself on my book, aptly describes the workings of my mind, underscoring the foolishness of its workings better from the outside than I could from the inside (I was moved). He accurately analyzes my mental state and, as I should point out, objectively and clearly dissects this state so as to bring out (appropriate) comic effects:

"The torment he [the 'he' being me] cannot escape," says Sartre, "is the same one he cannot bear. What if this torment is all that exists? If that is the case, it is precisely this torment he will attempt to falsify. The author himself admits it: 'I teach the art of turning anguish into delight.' And here is the trick involved: 'I know absolutely nothing.' Fine. This signifies that my knowledge stops—it goes no further. Beyond this is nothing, since nothing is the only thing I know. But what if I reify my ignorance? What if I transform it into the night of nonknowing? Suddenly it becomes positive: I can touch it, I can melt into it. 'When nonknowing is reached, absolute knowing becomes only "one knowing among others."' Better: I can feel very comfortable with it. There was light feebly illuminating this night, but for the present I have withdrawn into the night and it is *from the viewpoint of night* that I am considering the light. Nonknowing is a process of stripping bare. That proposition is a summit, but has to be understood in this way: stripped bare, therefore I *see* what knowing kept hidden till this point. But if I see, I *know*. I know indeed, but what I have known is again stripped bare by nonknowledge. If nonmeaning is meaning, the meaning that is nonmeaning is lost and becomes nonmeaning again (without any end to the process).' We won't catch our author napping. If he reifies nonknowing, it is with a certain wariness: in the manner of a movement, not a thing. And despite all, he pulls the trick off: the nonknowing that previously had not been *anything* is always becoming the beyond of knowing. Throwing himself forward, Mr. Bataille suddenly discovers himself *on the path to transcendence.* He has escaped. The disgust, shame, and nausea have remained behind with the knowing. Afterward there is little reason for his telling us, 'Nothing is revealed either in the fall or in the abyss.' For the essential is revealed, which is that my abjection is a nonmeaning and that there is a nonmeaning to this nonmeaning (which does not in any way revert to the original meaning). One of Mr. Blanchot's texts that Mr. Bataille quotes will reveal the deceit for us: 'The night soon seemed darker to him and more terrible than any other night, as if in fact it was coming from some wound, out of some thinking that had stopped being thinking, *out of thinking understood ironically as something other than thinking.*' Though, to be sure, Mr. Bataille refuses to see that nonknowing remains immanently in thinking. Thinking that thinks that it is not knowing remains thinking. It reveals the limitations of innerness but all the same does not give a general view. The equivalent would be to make nothing into something under the pretext of giving it a name. However, our author goes on to do just that. It is hardly that difficult for him. You and I, we might write 'I know nothing' quite sincerely. But let us assume that I enclose this *nothing* in quotation marks. Let us assume, like Mr. Bataille, I write: 'And above all it is "nothing," it is "nothing" that I know.' Here is a nothing that begins to look rather odd: it is detached and isolated, not far from having an existence on its own. For the present it will be enough to call it *the unknown* and the result will be attained. Nothing is what does not exist at all, and the unknown is what does not exist for me in any way. By naming nothing as the unknown, I turn it into an existence whose essence is to escape my knowing; and if I add that I know nothing, that signifies that I communicate with this existence in some other way than by knowing.

Here again Mr. Blanchot's text, referred to by our author, can be seen to shed some light for us: by means of this emptiness therefore 'the looking and the object of this looking blended together. Not only did the eye *which saw nothing* grasp something, but it grasped "the cause of its vision." *It saw as an object that which caused it not to see.*"* This, then, is the wild and free unknown to which Mr. Bataille sometimes gives and sometimes withholds the name of God. He has hypostasized pure nothingness. With a last effort of his, we will be dissolved ourselves in this night that till now has only protected us. Knowledge is what creates *an object* as over against a subject. Nonknowledge is 'a cancellation of subject and object, the only means of not ending up in a possession of an object by means of a subject.' There remains 'communication.' Which is to say, night absorbs everything. Now, Mr. Bataille forgets that with his own hands he has constructed a universal object—Night. So that it is time to apply to our author what Hegel said of Schelling's absolute, that at night all cows are black. It appears that to give oneself to the night is rapturous. I wouldn't doubt it. It is a certain way of dissolving oneself into *nothing*. But Mr. Bataille—as he did just a moment ago—satisfies his wish 'to be nothing' in a roundabout way. With the phrases 'nothing,' 'night,' and 'a nonknowing that lays bare' he has simply presented us with a fine little pantheistic ecstasy. I call to mind what Poincaré said of Riemanian geometry: replace the definition of the Riemanian plane with that of the Euclidian sphere, and you have Euclidian geometry. Indeed. And in similar fashion, Spinoza's system is pantheism of the right-handed type, while that of Mr. Bataille is the left-handed variety."

At this point, however, I am the one who should elucidate Sartre, instead of the other way around. He should have me say that it "*would be* a left-handed pantheism," if this infinite turbulence of mine had already ruled out even a possibility of stopping. Still, I can accept seeing myself from a standpoint that charges me with slowness of thought. Naturally in one form or another, I've myself observed these

---

* Sartre's emphasis.

inextricable difficulties to which Sartre refers: my thinking and its workings took these very difficulties as their starting point, though this was like a landscape glimpsed from a speeding train—what could be seen was always simply their dissolution into movement. I'd see them reborn in other shapes, accelerating at catastrophic speeds. So my principal impulse under these conditions was a disturbing awareness of giddiness. Peering into the very limits of existence, my headlong path forward, as it formed and reformed (opened and closed), never excluded awareness of the emptiness and foolishness of my thinking. But the pinnacle was the moment my intoxicating emptiness gave thinking a full consistency, a time in which, through the intoxication itself that it gave me, my nonmeaning took on the rights of meaning. If it intoxicates me, nonmeaning indeed has this meaning—*it intoxicates me*. And in that rapture it's correct to have loss of meaning, so it's the meaning of the fact of the loss of meaning. No sooner did the new meaning appear than it appeared as inconsistency—and nonmeaning again emptied me. But the return of nonmeaning was the departure of accumulated intoxication. While Sartre, never fazed and never intoxicated with any impulsiveness, judging my suffering and intoxication from the outside, without experiencing them, concludes this article of his by stressing the emptiness: "If the joys to which Mr. Bataille invites us," he says, "refer to themselves alone and are not integrated into a framework of new endeavors and don't contribute to forming a new humankind superseding itself toward new goals, they are equivalent to the pleasure of drinking a glass of spirits or feeling the sun's warmth at the beach." That is true, although I insist: specifically from the fact that that is what they are, specifically because I am left empty, they continue on within me as anguish. What I tried to describe in *Inner Experience* is a movement that as it loses any possibility of coming to a halt, falls easily under the attack of a criticism that thinks it can effect a halt from the outside, since this criticism itself isn't *caught* in that movement. My giddy fall and the *difference* it introduces into the mind can be grasped only by those experiencing it for themselves. Hence the possibility of reproaching me, as Sartre has done, first with leading readers to God and then with leading them to the void! These contradictory reproaches support my own assertion: *I don't lead anywhere.*

This is why criticism of my thought is difficult. Whatever might be said, my reply is given in advance, and for me significant criticism will only be a new means to anguish, with intoxication remaining the starting point. In the press of that headlong rush forward, comic as it was in so many ways, I never drew back: And Sartre has allowed me to start in again . . . There's no end to it.

But the following obvious weakness comes from the ease of that attitude:

"Life," I said, "is bound to be lost in death, as a river loses itself in the sea, the known in the unknown" (*Inner Experience*). And death is the end life easily reaches (as water does sea level). So why would I wish to turn my desire to be persuasive into a worry? I dissolve into myself like the sea—and I know the roaring waters of the torrent head straight at me! Whatever a judicious understanding sometimes seems to hide, an immense folly connected with it (understanding is only an infinitesimal part of that folly), doesn't hesitate to give back. The certainty of incoherence in reading, the inevitable crumbling of the soundest constructions, is the deep truth of books. Since appearance constitutes a limit, what truly exists is a dissolution into common opacity rather than a development of lucid thinking. The apparent unchangingness of books is deceptive: each book is also the sum of the misunderstandings it occasions.

So why exhaust myself with efforts toward consciousness? I can only make fun of myself as I write. (Why write even a phrase if laughter doesn't immediately join me?) It goes without saying that, for the task, I bring to bear whatever rigor I have within me. But the crumbling nature of thinking's awareness of itself and especially the certainty of thinking reaching its end only in failing, hinder any repose and prevent the relaxed state that facilitates a rigorous disposition of things. Committed to the casual stance—*I think and express myself in the free play of hazard.*

Obviously, everyone in some way admits the importance of hazard. But this recognition is as minimal and unconscious as possible. Going my way unconstrained, unhampered, I develop my thoughts, make choices with regard to expression—but I don't have the control over myself that I want. And the actual dynamic of my intelligence is equally uncontrollable. So that I owe to other dynamics—to lucky chance and to fleeting moments of relaxation—the minimal order and relative learning that I do have. And the rest of the time . . . Thus, as I see it my thought proceeds in harmony with its object, an object that it attains more and perfectly the greater the state of its own ruin. Though it isn't necessarily conscious of this. At one and the same time my thinking must reach plenary illumination and dissolution . . . In the same individual, thought must construct and destroy itself.

And even that isn't quite right. Even the most rigorous thinkers yield to chance. In addition, the demands inherent in the exercise of thought often take me far from where I started. One of the great difficulties encountered by understanding is to put order into thought's interrelations in time. In a given moment, my thought reaches considerable rigor. But how to link it with yesterday's thinking? Yesterday, in a sense, I was another person, responding to other worries. Adapting one to the other remains possible, but . . .

This insufficiency bothers me no more than the insufficiency relating to the many woes of the human condition generally. Humanness is related in us to nonsatisfaction, a nonsatisfaction to which we yield without accepting it, though; we distance ourselves from humanness when we regard ourselves as satisfied or when we give up searching for satisfaction. Sartre is right in relation to me to recall the *myth of Sisyphus*, though "in relation to me" here equates to "in relation to humanity," I suppose. What can be expected of us is to go as far as possible and not to stop. What by contrast, humanly speaking, can be *criticized* are endeavors whose only meaning is some relation to moments of completion. Is it possible for me to go further? I won't wait to coordinate my efforts in that case—I'll go further. I'll take the risk. And the reader, free not to venture after me, will often take advantage of that same freedom! The critics are right to scent danger here! But let me in turn point out a greater danger, one that comes from methods that, adequate only to an *outcome* of knowledge, confer on individuals whom they limit a sheerly *fragmentary existence*—an existence that is mutilated with respect to the *whole* that remains inaccessible.

Having recognized this, I'll defend my position.

I've spoken of *inner experience*: my intention was to make known an object. But by proposing this vague title, I didn't want to confine myself sheerly to inner facts of that experience. It's an arbitrary procedure to reduce knowledge to what we get from our intuitions as subjects. This is something only a newborn can do. And we ourselves (who write) can only know something about this newborn by observing it from outside (the child is only our object). A *separation* experience, related to a vital *continuum* (our conception and our birth) and to a return to that continuum (in our first sexual feelings and our first laughter), leaves us without any clear recollections, and only in objective operations do we reach the core of the being we are. A *phenomenology of the developed mind* assumes a coincidence of subjective and objective aspects and at the same time a fusion of subject and object.* This means an isolated operation is admissible only because of fatigue (so, the explanation I gave of laughter, because I was unable to develop a whole movement in tandem with a conjugation of the modalities of laughter would be left suspended—since every theory of laughter is integrally a philosophy and, similarly, every integral philosophy is a theory of laughter . . .). But that is the point—though I set forth these principles, at the same time I must renounce following them. Thought is produced in me as uncoordinated flashes, withdrawing endlessly from a term to which its movement pushes it. I can't tell if I'm expressing human helplessness this way, or my own . . . I don't know, though I'm not hopeful of even some outwardly satisfying outcome. Isn't there an advantage in creating philosophy as I do? A flash in the night—a language belonging to a brief moment . . . Perhaps in this respect this latest moment contains a simple truth.

In order to will knowledge, by an indirect expedient I tend to

---

* This is the fundamental requirement of Hegel's phenomenology. Clearly, instead of responding to it, modern phenomenology, while replying to changing human thought, is only one moment among others: a sandcastle, a mirage of sorts.

become the whole universe. But in this movement I can't be a whole human being, since I submit to a particular goal, becoming the whole. Granted, if I could become it, I would thus be a whole human being. But in my effort, don't I distance myself from exactly that? And how can I become the whole without becoming a whole human being? I can't be this whole human being except when I let go. I can't be this through willpower: my will necessarily has to will outcomes! But if misfortune (or chance) wills me to let go, then I know I am an integral, whole humanness, subordinate to nothing.

In other words, the moment of revolt inherent in willing a knowledge beyond practical ends can't be indefinitely continued. And in order to be the whole universe, humankind has to let go and abandon its principle, accepting as the sole criterion of what it is the tendency to go beyond what it is. This existence that I am is a revolt against existence and is indefinite *desire*. For this existence God was simply a stage—and now here he is, looming large, grown from unfathomable experience, comically perched on the stake used for impalement.

APPENDIX V
NOTHINGNESS, TRANSCENDENCE, IMMANENCE

My method has confusion as a consequence—and in the long run this confusion is unbearable (particularly for me!). This is something to be corrected if possible . . . But for now, I want to elucidate the meaning of the above words.

For me nothingness is a limit of an individual existence. Beyond its defined limits—in time and in space—this existence or being no longer exists, no longer is. For us, that nonbeing is filled with meaning: I know I can be reduced to nothing. Limited being is only a particular being. Although, does there exist such a thing as the totality of being (understood as the sum of beings)?

The transcendence of being is fundamentally this nothingness. When an object appears in the beyond of nothingness—in a certain sense, as a given fact of nothingness—that object transcends us.

Contrariwise, the more I grasp in some object the extension of an existence first revealed within myself, the more this object becomes immanent to me.

On the other hand, an object can be active. A real or unreal existence (a person, a god, or a state), by threatening others with death, heightens within itself its transcendent nature. Its essence is given to me in the nothingness that my limits define. Its very activity defines its limits. It is what is expressed in terms of nothingness; the figuration rendering it perceptible is that of superiority. If I want to ridicule it, I have to ridicule nothingness. Though, on the other hand, I ridicule this threatening existence when I ridicule nothingness. Laughter moves toward immanence, and in that nothingness is the object of laughter—but it is thus an object of a destruction.

Morality is transcendent insofar as it appeals to the good of a being constructed on the nothingness of our own existence (humanity given as sacred, the gods or God, the State).

If it turned out to be possible, a morality of the summit would demand the opposite situation—that I laugh at nothingness. But without doing it in the name of a superiority. If I let myself be killed for my country, I move toward the summit but don't attain it: I serve the good of my country, which is the beyond of my nothingness. If immanent morality were possible, it would have me die for no reason. But in the name of this nothing, it would demand my dying—in the name of the nothing that I ridicule! I laugh at it, and that demand disappears! If our duty was to die of laughter, the morality of this would be an impulse toward irrepressible laughter.

APPENDIX VI
SURREALISM AND TRANSCENDENCE

Having spoken (on p. 55) of André Breton, I should immediately have mentioned the debt I owe to Surrealism. If I've quoted anything to ill effect, it's against my own best interests.

The reader for whom "the letter" is less attractive than "the spirit" will notice in my questioning the continuation of a certain moral interrogation that permeated Surrealism and, in the climate presupposed by my life, a perhaps not unfamiliar prolongation of Surrealist intolerance. The possibility exists that in Breton's search for the object he goes astray. His concern for exteriority brings him up short when he arrives at transcendence. His method ties him to a position focused on *objects*, to which value belongs. He is forced by his decency to annihilate himself, to dedicate himself to the nothingness of objects and words. Nothingness is thus bogus: it sets up a play of competition, and nothingness subsists in the form of superiority. The Surrealist object is to be found essentially in aggression, its job being to annihilate or "reduce to nothingness." But this doesn't of course make it slavish, since its attacks have no reason or motive. It isn't any less effective, however, in bringing its author—whose will to immanence remains beyond question—into a play of transcendence.

Perhaps the movement expressed by Surrealism is now no longer focused on the object. It is, if you like, within my books (if I must say so myself, since who would see it otherwise?). Coming from a position of transcendent objects that confer an empty superiority on themselves in order to destroy, there develops a shift to immanence—and to all the magic of meditations. This is a more personal type of destruction—it is a stranger upheaval, a limitless questioning of self. Of the self and everything at the same time.

Index